W9-CCG-168

Readers' Response

Karen's husband was paralyzed in an accident over ten years ago. Jeannie is a single mom. Both women are Christians whose lives have known more than the average share of hardship. We asked them to read the manuscript, knowing that this was the real test of our book: Does it bring hope to those who long ago moved beyond clichés and canned answers? This is their response . . .

I found *The Sacred Romance* captivating. It's as if it has crept into my heart and pulled back the curtains to reveal a new, strange yet deeply drawing drama—a drama I hope and pray will become more my own. It is beautiful.

Karen Garland

The Sacred Romance is moving and deeply profound. I was caught off-guard, in a good way, by the level of transparency. I had the sense that I was reading something true, something penetrating, and something so heart-wrenchingly real I had to ask, *How have we missed this—how has this picture, this "story" eluded us so completely?* I guess because I felt I was reading the story for the very first time, even though I've heard it hundreds of times before.

Jeannie Crooks

Also from John Eldredge

The Journey of Desire

The Sacred Romance Workbook and Journal

Wild at Heart

Wild at Heart Field Manual

Dare to Desire

The Sacred
ROMANCE

Drawing Closer to the
Heart of God

BRENT CURTIS
and
JOHN ELDREDGE

NELSON BOOKS
A Division of Thomas Nelson Publishers
Since 1798
www.thomasnelson.com

Published in Nashville, Tennessee, by Thomas Nelson, Inc., and distributed in
Canada by Word Communications, Ltd., Richmond, British Columbia, and in
the United Kingdom by Word (UK), Ltd., Milton Keynes, England.

Library of Congress Cataloging-in-Publication Data

Curtis, Brent.
    The sacred romance: drawing closer to the heart of God / Brent Curtis
and John Eldredge.
        p. cm.
    ISBN 0-7852-7342-5 (pb)
    ISBN 0-7852-6723-9 (hc)
    1. Spiritual life. I. Title.
    BV4501.2.C866 1997
    248.4—dc21   97-180001
                                                                        CIP

Printed in the United States of America
05 06 07 08 QW 53 52

Contents

Acknowledgments

BRENT CURTIS: Any creative work is in some sense indebted to every person who has had an impact on one's life, for good or for bad. At this moment, I would like to thank some of those whose lives and hearts have contributed in special ways to what is written here.

I want to give much thanks to Jan and Sharon, my partner and my secretary, respectively, for their heartfelt suggestions and encouragement; my partner Laura for facing with me the loneliness of spiritual warfare; Randy Raysbrook, for sharing with me the fruit of his own exploration of the place of the heart in the spiritual life; and Bruce Nygren, for trusting John and me and for editing our work with a light hand.

To Ralph and Isaac, who have walked with me in different times and on different legs of the journey as brothers of the heart—you have impacted my life in eternal ways; and to John, whose heart and courage in pursuing God flow through the pages of this book intermingled with my own—I thank God for each of you.

To my sisters, Candy, Angelita, and Brenda, and my brother, Donnie: The years of growing up have mingled your joys, sorrows, and struggles with my own in ways that are with me always. To you, Mom, for always wanting our best; and to Paul, Don, and my own father, Frederick—from each of you I learned something about being a man.

To you, Drew and Ben, for all the times of "block from the

hallway," prison tag, wrestling, and laughing at silly things. I love you both with all my heart and pray this book will be a window on the deepest thing that has guided my own life's journey. As well, may it be a light and a compass, part of guiding your own way home to the Lord Jesus Christ, who gave you to Mom and me out of his love.

Last, to you, Ginny, for loaning me your eyes and heart in reading the manuscript and for your patience over the years with my rough edges. Remember the black sand beach in New En-gland and the wedding ring captured on the last pull of the rake? In anticipation and hope, I dedicate this book to you.

JOHN ELDREDGE: Thanks to you, Dad, for teaching me to fish, introducing me to the West, and for our years together on the water and in the woods. And to you, Mom, for introducing me to the theater, to Shakespeare, and literature; and to both of you, for your love to me.

Thanks to you, Brent, for the idea of this book and for the immense courage and grace it took to collaborate.

Thanks to my wife, Stasi, whose great heart has been to mine an inspiration beyond words, love too deep for telling. I dedicate this book to you.

And from both of us, our gratitude and heartfelt love to Jesus of Nazareth, Author and Finisher of the Sacred Romance.

1

The Lost Life of the Heart

*Thirsty hearts are those whose longings have been
wakened by the touch of God within them.*
                                        A. W. Tozer

SOME YEARS into our spiritual journey, after the waves
of anticipation that mark the beginning of any pilgrimage have begun to ebb into life's middle years of service and busyness, a voice speaks to us in the midst of all we are
doing. *There is something missing in all of this*, it suggests. *There
is something more.*

The voice often comes in the middle of the night or the
early hours of morning, when our hearts are most unedited and
vulnerable. At first, we mistake the source of this voice and
assume it is just our imagination. We fluff up our pillow, roll
over, and go back to sleep. Days, weeks, even months go by and
the voice speaks to us again: *Aren't you thirsty? Listen to your
heart. There is something missing.*

We listen and we are aware of . . . a sigh. And under the sigh
is something dangerous, something that feels adulterous and
disloyal to the religion we are serving. We sense a passion deep
within that threatens a total disregard for the program we are
living; it feels reckless, wild. Unsettled, we turn and walk
quickly away, like a woman who feels more than she wants to
when her eyes meet those of a man not her husband.

1

We tell ourselves that this small, passionate voice is an intruder who has gained entry because we have not been diligent enough in practicing our religion. Our pastor seems to agree with this assessment and exhorts us from the pulpit to be more faithful. We try to silence the voice with outward activity, redoubling our efforts at Christian service. We join a small group and read a book on establishing a more effective prayer life. We train to be part of a church evangelism team. We tell ourselves that the malaise of spirit we feel even as we step up our religious activity is a sign of spiritual immaturity and we scold our heart for its lack of fervor.

Sometime later, the voice in our heart dares to speak to us again, more insistently this time. *Listen to me—there is something missing in all this. You long to be in a love affair, an adventure. You were made for something more. You know it.*

When the young prophet Samuel heard the voice of God calling to him in the night, he had the counsel from his priestly mentor, Eli, to tell him how to respond. Even so, it took them three times to realize it was God calling. Rather than ignoring the voice, or rebuking it, Samuel finally listened.

In our modern, pragmatic world we often have no such mentor, so we do not understand it is God speaking to us in our heart. Having so long been out of touch with our deepest longing, we fail to recognize the voice and the One who is calling to us through it. Frustrated by our heart's continuing sabotage of a dutiful Christian life, some of us silence the voice by locking our heart away in the attic, feeding it only the bread and water of duty and obligation until it is almost dead, the voice now small and weak. But sometimes in the night, when our defenses are down, we still hear it call to us, oh so faintly—a distant whisper. Come morning, the new day's activities scream for our attention, the sound of the cry is gone, and we congratulate ourselves on finally overcoming the flesh.

Others of us agree to give our heart a life on the side if it will only leave us alone and not rock the boat. We try to lose ourselves in our work, or "get a hobby" (either of which soon begin to feel like an addiction); we have an affair, or develop a colorful fantasy life fed by dime-store romances or pornography. We learn to enjoy the juicy intrigues and secrets of gossip. We make sure to maintain enough distance between ourselves and others, and even between ourselves and our own heart, to keep hidden the practical agnosticism we are living now that our inner life has been divorced from our outer life. Having thus appeased our heart, we nonetheless are forced to give up our spiritual journey because our heart will no longer come with us. It is bound up in the little indulgences we feed it to keep it at bay.

Losing Heart

The life of the heart is a place of great mystery. Yet we have many expressions to help us express this flame of the human soul. We describe a person without compassion as "heartless," and we urge him or her to "have a heart." Our deepest hurts we call "heartaches." Jilted lovers are "brokenhearted." Courageous soldiers are "bravehearted." The truly evil are "blackhearted" and saints have "hearts of gold." If we need to speak at the most intimate level, we ask for a "heart-to-heart" talk. "Lighthearted" is how we feel on vacation. And when we love someone as truly as we may, we love "with all our heart." But when we lose our passion for life, when a deadness sets in which we cannot seem to shake, we confess, "My heart's just not in it."

In the end, it doesn't matter how well we have performed or what we have accomplished—a life without heart is not worth living. For out of this wellspring of our soul flows all true caring and all meaningful work, all real worship and all sacrifice. Our faith, hope, and love issue from this fount, as well. Because it is in our heart that we first hear the voice of God and it is in the heart that we come to know him and learn to live in his love.

So you can see that to lose heart is to lose everything. And a "loss of heart" best describes most men and women in our day. It isn't just the addictions and affairs and depression and heartaches, though, God knows, there is enough of these to cause even the best of us to lose heart. But there is the busyness, the drivenness, the fact that most of us are living merely to survive. Beneath it we feel restless, weary, and vulnerable.

Indeed, the many forces driving modern life have not only assaulted the life of our heart, they have also dismantled the heart's habitat—that geography of mystery and transcendence we knew so well as children.

I (Brent) remember sitting in my college zoology class as my professor expounded with upraised arms—the perspiration-stained underarms of his shirt proudly exposed—that man's basic problem was that he wanted to smell (be) like a flower instead of a mammal. In physics class, the professor seemed to take satisfaction in explaining to us that the beauty of sunsets and rainbows was due only to the refraction of light through water and dust particles in the air. It was as if the miracle of light itself were somehow done away with by these explanations. I remember leaving those professors of the Age of Reason with a sense of loss, a sense of "Oh, so that's all it is." The message of my teachers was clear: Once we dispense with unhelpful mysticism and superstition, the progress of mankind will proceed unhindered.

All of us have had that experience at one time or another, whether it be as we walked away from our teachers, our parents, a church service, or sexual intimacy; the sense that something important, perhaps the only thing important, had been explained away or tarnished and lost to us forever. Sometimes little by little, sometimes in large chunks, life has appropriated the terrain meant to sustain and nourish the more wild life of the heart, forcing it to retreat as an endangered species into smaller, more secluded, and often darker geographies for its survival. As this has happened, something has been lost, something vital.

For what shall we do when we wake one day to find we have lost touch with our heart and with it the very refuge where God's presence resides?

Starting very early, life has taught all of us to ignore and distrust the deepest yearnings of our heart. Life, for the most part, teaches us to suppress our longing and live only in the external world where efficiency and performance are everything. We have learned from parents and peers, at school, at work, and even from our spiritual mentors that something else is wanted from us other than our heart, which is to say, that which is most deeply *us.* Very seldom are we ever invited to live out of our heart. If we are wanted, we are often wanted for what we can offer functionally. If rich, we are honored for our wealth; if beautiful, for our looks, if intelligent, for our brains. So we learn to offer only those parts of us that are approved, living out a carefully crafted performance to gain acceptance from those who represent life to us. We divorce ourselves from our heart and begin to live a double life. Frederick Buechner expresses this phenomenon in his biographical work, *Telling Secrets.*

> "[Our] original shimmering self gets buried so deep we hardly live out of it at all . . . rather, we learn to live out of all the other selves which we are constantly putting on and taking off like coats and hats against the world's weather."

On the outside, there is the external story of our lives. This is the life everyone sees, our life of work and play and church, of family and friends, paying bills, and growing older. Our external story is where we carve out the identity most others know. It is the place where we have learned to label each other in a way that implies we have reached our final destination. Bob is an accountant; Mary works for the government; Ted is an attorney. The Smiths are the family with the well-kept lawn and lovely children; the Joneses are that family whose children are always in trouble. Here, busyness substitutes for meaning, efficiency substitutes for creativity, and functional relationships substitute for love. In the outer life we live from *ought* (I ought to do this) rather than from *desire* (I want to do this) and management substitutes for mystery. There are three steps to a happy marriage, five ways to improve your portfolio, and seven habits for success.

There *is* a spiritual dimension to this external world in our desire to do good works, but communion with God is replaced by activity for God. There is little time in this outer world for deep questions. Given the right plan, everything in life can be managed . . . except your heart.

The inner life, the story of our heart, is the life of the deep places within us, our passions and dreams, our fears and our deepest wounds. It is the unseen life, the mystery within—what Buechner calls our "shimmering self." It cannot be managed like a corporation. The heart does not respond to principles and programs; it seeks not efficiency, but passion. Art, poetry, beauty, mystery, ecstasy: These are what rouse the heart. Indeed, they are the language that must be spoken if one wishes to communicate with the heart. It is why Jesus so often taught and related to people by telling stories and asking questions. His desire was not just to engage their intellects but to capture their hearts.

Indeed, if we will listen, a Sacred Romance calls to us through our heart every moment of our lives. It whispers to us on the wind, invites us through the laughter of good friends, reaches out to us through the touch of someone we love. We've heard it in our favorite music, sensed it at the birth of our first child, been drawn to it while watching the shimmer of a sunset on the ocean. The Romance is even present in times of great personal suffering: the illness of a child, the loss of a marriage, the death of a friend. Something calls to us through experiences like these and rouses an inconsolable longing deep within our heart, wakening in us a yearning for intimacy, beauty, and adventure.

This longing is the most powerful part of any human personality. It fuels our search for meaning, for wholeness, for a sense of being truly alive. However we may describe this deep desire, it is the most important thing about us, our heart of hearts, the passion of our life. And the voice that calls to us in this place is none other than the voice of God.

We cannot hear this voice if we have lost touch with our heart.

The true story of every person in this world is not the story you see, the external story. The true story of each person is the journey of his or her heart. Jesus himself knew that if people lived only in the outer story, eventually they would lose track of their inner life, the life of their heart he so much desired to redeem. Indeed, it was to the most religious people of his time that Jesus spoke his strongest warnings about a loss of heart.

It is tragic for any person to lose touch with the life of their heart but especially so for those of us who once heard the call in our heart and recognized it as the voice of Jesus of Nazareth. We may remember him inviting us to a life of beauty, intimacy, and adventure that we thought was lost. For others of us, when he called, it felt for the first time in our lives as if our heart had finally found a home. We responded in faith, in hope, and in love and began the journey we call the Christian life. Each day seemed a new adventure as we rediscovered the world with God by our side.

But for many of us, the waves of first love ebbed away in the whirlwind of Christian service and activity, and we began to lose the Romance. Our faith began to feel more like a series of problems that needed to be solved or principles that had to be mastered before we could finally enter into the abundant life

voice communing with us when he comes to call us more deeply to the Romance he has set within us.

It is possible to recover the lost life of our heart and with it the intimacy, beauty, and adventure of life with God. To do so we must leave what is familiar and comfortable—perhaps even parts of the religion in which we have come to trust—and take a journey. This journey first takes us on a search for the lost life of our heart, and for the voice that once called us in those secret places; those places and times when our heart was still with us. The pilgrimage of the heart leads us to remember together what it was that first engaged us in deep ways as children: ". . . anyone who will not receive the kingdom of God like a little child will never enter it," said Jesus (Mark 10:15).

Our journey will take us to explore the hidden questions of our heart, born out of the stories of our lives. It is only by leaving home and taking a pilgrimage that we will begin to see how our own stories are interwoven with the great Romance God has been telling since before the dawn of time. It is on this pilgrimage that we begin to see that each of us has a part in the cosmic love affair that was created specifically with us in mind. Last, this pilgrimage brings us to the destination, set within all of our hearts, which in some way we have known, longed for, and been haunted by since we were children.

This book is born out of the journey that John and I have shared for several years. I have been a Christian counselor for the same length of time that John has been conducting seminars for a major Christian ministry. Both of us have at one time worked in a local church. Our lives have given us a unique look into the inner life of modern Christianity, and what we have known from our own stories has been confirmed again and again through hundreds of encounters with other believers: Most Christians have lost the life of their heart and with it, their romance with God. As we trace the steps of the journey toward God's resurrection of the heart, we hope to help you discover your soul's deepest longing and invite you to embrace it as the most important part of your life.

It is our aim to help you "guard your heart," to see more clearly the enemies of your heart and the hearts of those you love; to enable you to better enter the battle for hearts to which our Captain calls us.

Our journey begins by asking questions, putting words to the movements of the heart. "What is this restlessness and emptiness I feel, sometimes long years into my Christian journey? What does the spiritual life have to do with the rest of my life? What is it that is set so deeply in my heart, experienced as a longing for adventure and romance, that simply will not leave me alone? Does it have anything to do with God? What is it that he wants from me? Has he been speaking to me through my heart all along? When did I stop listening? When did his voice first call to me?"

2

An Unknown Romancing

We wake, if ever we wake at all, to mystery.
Annie Dillard

WHAT, OR WHO, first calls to us from the wellspring of our heart? Our external stories, the ones we live in front of the world, filled with busyness and bustle, will not give us the answer to our question. We must move to the internal story that goes on in our heart. If we are going to begin the journey toward the recovery of our heart, we must follow Frederick Buechner's advice and "listen to our lives."

> If God speaks to us at all other than through such official channels as the Bible and the church, then I think that he speaks to us largely through what happens to us . . . if we keep our hearts and minds open as well as our ears, if we listen with patience and hope, if we remember at all deeply and honestly, then I think we come to recognize, beyond all doubt, that, however faintly we may hear him, he is indeed speaking to us, and that, however little we may understand of it, his word to each of us is both recoverable and precious beyond telling. (*Now and Then*)

Our inner story is most audible early in the morning, or sometimes in the middle of the night when the inner editor that tells us how we "should" respond to the world has gone off duty. It is then that our heart speaks to us of the story that is most deeply ours. It is a story whose plot contains both mystery

and magic as well as foreboding and anxiety—what philosophers call "angst." When we listen most attentively to the inner
story our heart tells us about, most of us are aware that the plot
revolves around two very different messages, or revelations, that
have vied for our attention since we were very young. One has
enchanted us while the other has dared us to rise above fear and
resignation. The first has come to us in the form of a romancing that even now in my forties often fills me (Brent) with anticipation. Something wonderful woos us. The other lays siege to
us in much darker hues and brings with it a foreboding that
sometimes nags at the edges of our consciousness even on the
most sunlit morning. Something fearful stalks us.

And yet, life's enchantment of us is, perhaps, the deeper of
the two messages—the love story that first engaged our heart
before the darker revelation did its work. And so it is here we
will begin to "listen to our lives." If we will allow ourselves to
go back to the story most of us knew as children, it is not hard
to bring back the early images and sounds and aromas of life's
first revelation—that of a great Romance.

Each of us has a geography where the Romance first spoke
to us. It is usually the place we both long to see again and fear
returning to for fear our memories will be stolen from us. My
own earliest memories of the Romance come from 120 acres of
New Jersey farmland, bordered by a stream to the southeast and
a low and broad hillside to the northwest. As was the case with
most family farms in the 1950s, the labor of both my mother
and father was required by the animals and fields from early
morning to dusk, leaving my sister and me to explore the mysteries of meadows and haymows.

I first remember the Romance calling to me when I was a
boy of six or seven, just past dusk on a summer evening, when
the hotter and dustier work of the farm had given way to
another song. Something warm and alive and poignantly haunting would call to me from the mysterious borders of the farm

that was my world. I would walk toward it, past the corrals where our milk cows rested, down through rows of dark green corn that towered far over my head. The corn, imperious in its height and numbers, presented its own kind of enchanted forest. Every leaf that gave way before my outstretched arms offered possible mystery. The earth was warm and brown and fragrant and seemed to invite a sort of barefooted ecstasy with no worry of stones or other debris to cause me harm.

Finally I would come to the end of the corn out into a fringe of meadow where tall grasses swayed in silvery response to the moonlight's embrace. Beyond these dancers a thin line of maple and oak trees, straight as sentinels, hid the voices calling so passionately to me from moving water where the creek formed the border of our farm. The hardwoods that guarded the creek would usher me to a sandbar below an old wooden bridge that carried the road above on into New Jersey's rich farmlands. There in the moonlight, I would squat down on my heels near the water's edge, letting my toes sink into the cool sand. Around the imprint of my foot, the sand would bleed the deep reds of rusting iron ore.

In that place I was in the middle of the singers.

The voices of crickets, katydids, and cicadas would come to me, carried above the sounds of the creek and mingled with the pungent odor of tannins. Tens of thousands of stream-side musicians sang to me the magic stories of the farms and forests. It seemed as if the songs were carried all the way from the headwaters—those mysterious beginnings of the waters that came up through the mosses and cattails in a manner no less magical than if they had been called to life by moon-dusted fairies. The creek waters would rest in the darkness under the bridge before continuing their journey. The surface stillness of the resulting pond played host to the shiny green lords of the young river, the deep-throated bullfrogs. They added their own intermittent bass notes to the melody; a call to order unheeded by the great mass of musicians.

I remember being in that place until the music of life would fill me with the knowledge of some Romance to be lived; an assurance that there was a reason to joust against dragons with wooden swords; a reason to wear not one but two pearl-handled revolvers in the cowboy stories I weaved and lived out each day; a reason to include a pretty girl who needed to be rescued, even though I was far too busy fighting the bad guys to be captured by love. The magic assured me of loves and lovers and adventures to be joined and mystery to be pursued.

The Romance of that place would surround me as I rose and returned through the cornfield in response to my mother's distant call. It comforted me with a familiarity that seemed to connect me with things that were at once very old and still becoming new. Lying on my bed, with my parents far off downstairs in another part of the house and a geography of the heart I did not then know, I would fall asleep, romanced by some unseen lover that, back then, I only knew from those singers in the summer moonlit night.

I, perhaps like you, have encountered the Romance many times since: in the golden fall of the Rockies and in the windswept sea grasses and whitecaps of bay and ocean on the Atlantic; in a quiet moment of sunlight orchestrated into parallel rays of warmth on my shoulder as I read a good book; in the eyes of certain women and the strength of certain men; in the joy of my five-year-old son turning cartwheels during a soccer game, oblivious to the demands of winning; and in rare occurrences of kindness, courage, and sacrifice by men and women I have known and reports of the same by many I have not.

In my adult years it has ebbed and flowed and usually comes as a surprise. One vivid appearance took place perhaps four years ago on a summer's evening. A couple who were longtime friends of ours before we moved to Colorado were visiting us from the East Coast. It was a difficult time for them individually and for their marriage. This particular night the four of us had gone to see *When Harry Met Sally*, a poignant comedy-drama on the subject of whether men and women could just be friends. The movie provoked much emotion in our friends and they walked down to the lake near our home to talk about their hurt and anger and their future. Our house sits on a ridge in the southern portion of our city and my wife and I sat at the table in our darkened dining room, looking out at the lights of surrounding neighborhoods.

I felt heavy and sad inside over the pain of our friends. Heavy about the unknown future of their marriage and our friendship. Sad as well at some of the distances in our own marriage that had rarely been bridged. As I put these things into words with Ginny, she reached out and took my hand. I don't remember the exact words of our conversation, but I remember her sitting there in a summer dress with her blue eyes visible even in the twilight. I know we talked about being a man and being a woman and what it was like to love and be in love. I felt as if some veil that was often suspended between us fell away for a few moments and we talked as friends. Friends who had the possibility of deeper romance.

I remember going to bed that night feeling much the same as I felt as a boy on those summer nights so long ago, stirred and enchanted by a taste of beauty and intimacy that came by surprise. The tears I shed in the moments before sleep were sad and joyous and felt not at all contradictory. When I awoke the next morning I reached for the sense of the Romance inside but I knew it was gone before I even went into the kitchen for coffee. The veil had dropped back into place and the day before me seemed to offer only the everyday responsibilities of job and family and simply going on.

Remembering these scenes from my own story, I realized that I had found part of the lost journey of my heart. As a young boy, my heart was captured by mystery: mystery that invited me to open my heart and join it in a kind of joyful exuberance; mystery that hinted of a story that existed on its own outside my own fanciful creations; a story that nonetheless invited me to be part of it as I constructed my childhood adventures; a story that offered me villains and heroes and a story line that evolved out of their conflict; a story that, along with telling me of great danger, also told me that all things would be well; a story that felt as if it began in laughter and was confident that it would bring all who were a part of it home in joyful communion.

Sadly, many of us never come to see this wooing, in whatever geography it first finds us, as having anything to do with our heart's deepest desire, our spiritual life, or our soul's destiny. This is true in part because it is a story that is very hard to capture in propositions. We have learned to tell ourselves that it is naive to trust it after we become adults, as if somehow we have outgrown it and moved on to more reasonable or "scientific" ways of thinking. We have learned to think of it as quaint, or sentimental, or the foolishness of a child. Contemporary Christianity has often taught us to mistrust it, for fear it will lead us into some New Age heresy, unwittingly giving away what most deeply belongs to Christian faith. We are certainly rarely told to listen to it, look for it, follow it to its source.

Thankfully, our heart will not totally give up on the Romance. In spite of our "maturity" or the admonitions of our teachers to avoid the "things of this world," we find ourselves with a lump in our throat at a movie when two lovers we know are meant to be together finally find each other—or don't. Another movie tells the story of a man with a noble heart. He sacrifices comfort and safety for a cause higher than mere political expediency. He is defeated, yet his spirit enthralls us with his heroism. We leave the theater with a burning in our heart; a desire to be part of such a cause.

In all of our hearts lies a longing for a Sacred Romance.

It will not go away in spite of our efforts over the years to anesthetize or ignore its song, or attach it to a single person or endeavor. It is a Romance couched in mystery and set deeply within us. It cannot be categorized into propositional truths or fully known any more than studying the anatomy of a corpse would help us know the person who once inhabited it.

Philosophers call this Romance, this heart yearning set within us, the longing for transcendence; the desire to be part of something larger than ourselves, to be part of something out of the ordinary that is good. Transcendence is what we experience in a small but powerful way when our city's football team wins the big game against tremendous odds. The deepest part of our heart longs to be bound together in some heroic purpose with others of like mind and spirit.

Indeed, if we reflect back on the journey of our heart, the Romance has most often come to us in the form of two deep desires: the longing for adventure that *requires* something of us, and the desire for intimacy—to have someone truly know us for ourselves, while at the same time inviting us to *know* them in the naked and discovering way lovers come to know each other on the marriage bed. The emphasis is perhaps more on adventure for men and slightly more on intimacy for women. Yet, both desires are strong in us as men and women. In the words of friends, these two desires come together in us all as a longing to be in a relationship of heroic proportions.

When I was a boy, I loved to jump from our haymow onto the backs of steers feeding at the hayrack directly underneath. The ensuing bareback ride was always an adventure of the highest order. I also loved to watch *The Mickey Mouse Club* on television, just to have a moment's intimacy with Annette (Funicello). I am still partly convinced our eyes met a time or two and she smiled at me. These two boyhood passions for adventure and intimacy often came together in my fantasies in a story in which I would rescue Annette from the bad guys and escape with her into the mountains where we would live happily ever after. I would be her hero. She would be my beauty. And we would always be ready to fight the bad guys again whenever the world needed us, side by side.

Whatever form each of our intimate adventures has taken in our fantasies, or in "real life," this Sacred Romance is set within all our hearts and will not go away. It is the core of our spiritual journey. Any religion that ignores it survives only as guilt-induced legalism, a set of propositions to be memorized and rules to be obeyed.

Someone or something has romanced us from the beginning with creek-side singers and pastel sunsets, with the austere majesty of snowcapped mountains and the poignant flames of autumn colors telling us of something—or someone—leaving, with a promise to return. These things can, in an unguarded moment, bring us to our knees with longing for this something or someone who is lost; someone or something only our heart recognizes. C. S. Lewis knew this longing well:

> Even in your hobbies, has there not always been some secret attraction which the others are curiously ignorant of—something, not to be identified with, but always on the verge of breaking through, the smell of cut wood in the workshop or the clap-clap of water against the boat's side? Are not all lifelong friendships born at the moment when at last you meet another human being who has some inkling (but faint and uncertain even in the best) of that something which you were born desiring, and which, beneath the flux of other desires and in all the momentary silences between the louder passions, night and day, year by year, from childhood to old age, you are looking for, watching for, listening for? You have never *had* it. All the things that have ever deeply possessed your soul have been but hints of it—tantalizing glimpses, promises never quite fulfilled, echoes that died away just as they caught your ear. But if it should really become manifest—if there ever came an echo that did

not die away but swelled into the sound itself—you would know it. Beyond all possibility of doubt you would say, "Here at last is the thing I was made for." We cannot tell each other about it. It is the secret signature of each soul, the incommunicable and unappeasable want, the thing we desired before we met our wives or made our friends or chose our work, and which we shall still desire on our deathbeds, when the mind no longer knows wife or friend or work. While we are, this is. If we lose this, we lose all.

Indeed, art, literature, and music have all portrayed and explored the Romance, or its loss, in myriad scenes, images, sounds, and characters that nonetheless speak to us out of the same story. The universality of the story is the reason Shakespeare's plays, even though they speak to us from a pastoral setting in England across four hundred years of time, speak so eloquently and faithfully that they are still performed on stages from Tokyo to New York City.

It is as if someone has left us with a haunting in our innerheart stories that will not go away; nor will it allow itself to be captured and ordered. The Romance comes and goes as it wills. And so we are haunted by it.

What does this Romance have to do with God? Could it be that the more literal, propositional message of Christianity that we recite to each other in the Apostles' Creed is the same secret message those singers were sharing with each other and with me on those long-ago summer evenings of my boyhood? Has God left us all with the haunting of this Sacred Romance to draw us toward home?

If this poignant longing were the only deep experience of our soul, then we should not lose heart. Though we may not have tasted satisfaction yet, we would search for it all our lives. There are enough hints and clues and "tantalizing glimpses" to keep us searching, our heart ever open and alive to the quest. But there is another message that comes to all of us in varying shades and intensities, even in our early years. It often seems to come out of nowhere and for no discernible reason that we can fathom. It is dark, powerful, and full of dread. I think of it as the Message of the Arrows.

3

The Message of the Arrows

I cried when I was born and every day shows why.
George Herbert

THERE ARE ONLY TWO THINGS that pierce the human heart, wrote Simone Weil. One is beauty. The other is affliction. And while we wish there were only beauty in the world, each of us has known enough pain to raise serious doubts about the universe we live in. From very early in life we know another message, warning us that the Romance has an enemy.

The psalmist speaks of this enemy and tells us we need not fear it:

> He [God] will save you from the fowler's snare
>   and from the deadly pestilence.
> He will cover you with his feathers,
>   and under his wings you will find refuge;
>   his faithfulness will be your shield and rampart.
> You will not fear the terror of night,
>   nor the arrow that flies by day. *(Ps. 91:3–5)*

Yet we cannot deny that the Arrows have struck us all, sometimes arriving in a hail of projectiles that blocked out the sun, and other times descending in more subtle flight that only let us know we were wounded years later, when the wound festered and broke.

23

One of the first Arrows I (Brent) remember came on a fall morning when the green choruses of summer were no longer there to comfort me. I happened upon my mother standing by the stove one morning before school began, stirring oatmeal. She had been crying and the tears still welled up in her eyes. They were not the kind of tears shed in anger or even pain due to a momentary spat with my father. They were not due to some recently delivered message about illness or death in the family.

They were the tears of a frightened girl in her mid-twenties who could find no meeting place between the life she found herself living as wife and mother and the needs of her own wounded heart that never felt the connection with mother and father so necessary to living with courage and hope. I couldn't have put that into words back then, but I felt the fear as a palpable enemy that needed to be quickly defeated. If there was an adversary of the heart that even adults did not know how to handle, my world was much less safe than I had thought. I moved quickly to help my mother vanquish this foe in the best way I knew how.

I think I put my hand on her arm and said something like, "It will be all right." I remember feeling a separation within myself and from her even then that kept me from addressing her as Mom or Mommy. I didn't understand that the arrows were already inside both of us. She looked angry that anyone could believe anything so foolish and said something like, "It's not all right. You kids just don't know what it's like."

My stepfather was not there to show me how to fend off Arrows such as these and so they entered into me and, as I later came to know, lodged in a deep place. Still later, I came to realize he did not know how to defeat the enemy either, for himself or me.

This other Message of the Arrows that I learned on fall and winter mornings seemed as strong and often stronger than the message of those summer creek-side singers. I remember sitting in the school cafeteria alone, trying to pull the Arrows out or at least cover them over so I could enter into the banter that seemed to flow so easily from my friends. I remember being pinned down on the playground by a friend of mine who was bigger than me and feeling that I would always be in that place if I wasn't careful.

I remember standing in the kitchen of our old farmhouse in my pajamas one morning at the age of five or six when two men in felt hats and long overcoats came to ask where my parents were. They asked several questions, all of which I answered, "I don't know." Finally they turned in disgust and said in parting, "You don't know much, do you, kid?"

There were other Arrows over the years that struck in that same deep place. Arrows that carried messages about ears that were too big, and a father who never called or wrote; my step-father, who was a cowboy, commenting to my mother that I was a town kid; another stepfather who came and went and never stayed in touch. There was a girl I loved but couldn't love (intimacy requires a heart that is released and mine was pinned down with unknown fears and grief) and so I let her go; and total confusion over what vocation I would pursue or even had any ability for. The Arrows flew and all seemed to strike close to that fearful place, a place that said that I was alone in a coldly indifferent world. And even the ones that didn't, I made sure they ended up there. I needed the message to be at least consistent that the world was clearly a fearful place.

I remember, one day in winter in my early twenties, going back to stand on the bridge over that same creek that had been so magical for me as a boy. It was two years after returning home from college. I had spent most of five years there still pursuing the Romance through parties, alcohol, and drugs, and in always making sure I was present when anything was going on. I feared that if I missed any opportunity, the magic would come while I was not there and I would miss it forever. And for a time, the Arrows seemed to be silenced by the endless possibility that "something *was* about to happen." College life hid so much disappointment behind the illusion that life hadn't really started yet. The Arrows remained silent until a disinterested office worker placed my diploma in my hand without looking up and I found myself standing on the front steps of my college administrative offices with no more reason to stay.

The Message of the Arrows

I had graduated from college without finding a love or a vocation. The adults I knew (who so often try to fill emptiness of soul with economic solutions) told me it was time to settle down and find a responsible life. I, on the other hand, felt that I had only begun to be restless. I felt there was nowhere I really belonged or even wanted to belong; that whatever story my family and friends had found to live in, my own had become a succession of meaningless chapters with no plot other than filling in the days. It was a longing for the landscape of those summer evenings of so long ago that called me again to the bridge that day. It was a hope that I would find some clarity of vision in the place I had loved so much as a boy.

I stood there that November day looking down onto a small, brown stream bordered in lifeless gray hardwoods and monochromatic fallen leaves. The waters themselves flowed listlessly over the barriers of leaves and sticks in their path, as if wearied by the constant chore of movement. In many places, the dams built by the winter debris stilled their life with little resistance. A few hundred yards off to my right stood our old farmhouse, now vacant with a large hole in the roof. The barns and sheds and corrals that had given it a reason to exist were gone. Weeds grew in a tangled confusion where the corn had once stood in ordered wildness. The weariness of it all came together in the silence of those absent August songsters from so many years ago.

I remember feeling a sharp pain in my chest that I silenced with cold anger. I thought what a fool I had been all these years to believe in the summer message of this place. Laid out before me in the light of day was obviously the reality that had always been there. It was time I stopped believing a lie. The mysterious Love and Lover that had come to me in my childhood were frauds.

I know now I placed that last Arrow in my heart that day and shoved it cleanly through. I did it to kill the tears of mourning inside that would have insisted that there was something I had lost. Yet the Haunting was still there that day on the bridge. I only understood years later that it was I myself who killed it— or tried to. If I had allowed the loss I felt to flow in the waters of my own tears, the haunting call of that long-ago summer would have remained. It was in placing a dam of hardness over the ache I felt inside that I refused to acknowledge the Haunting and even misinterpreted the message of autumn: Something Lost and Again Coming.

At some point we all face the same decision—what will we do with the Arrows we've known? Maybe a better way to say it is, what have they tempted us to do? However they come to us, whether through a loss we experience as abandonment or some deep violation we feel as abuse, their message is always the same: Kill your heart. Divorce it, neglect it, run from it, or indulge it with some anesthetic (our various addictions). Think of how you've handled the affliction that has pierced your own heart. How did the Arrows come to you? Where did they land? Are they still there? What have you done as a result?

To say we all face a decision when we're pierced by an Arrow is misleading. It makes the process sound so rational, as though we have the option of coolly assessing the situation and choosing a logical response. Life isn't like that—the heart cannot be managed in a detached sort of way (certainly not when we are young, when some of the most defining Arrows strike). It feels more like an ambush and our response is at a gut level. We may never put words to it. Our deepest convictions are formed without conscious effort, but the effect is a shift deep in our soul. Commitments form never to be in that position again, never to know that sort of pain again. The result is an approach to life that we often call our personality. If you'll listen carefully to your life, you may begin to see how it has been shaped by the unique Arrows you've known and the particular convictions you've embraced as a result. The Arrows also taint and partially direct even our spiritual life.

My own spiritual journey with Christ "began" (I've since come to know the beginning was long before I was born) when my first prayer to God since I was a boy escaped from my heart one morning at work. It was the morning after another night of searching for something or someone; searching in bars, nightclubs, and just driving the roads listening to music all with the help of enough alcohol and drugs to keep the search hopeful. I was working, installing pipe in the bottom of sewer wells. I and the men I worked with lived with a cynicism that did for us in daylight hours what the alcohol and drugs did at night. We wryly commented to each other, standing in sewage up to our chests at four in the morning, that we were as far down in life as we could get, and there was no way to go but up.

One morning, almost without my bidding, my heart cried out from its own depths, "God, help me, because I am lost." And God answered with lavish faithfulness in those "first-love" years. I began reading the Bible and it came alive in my hands and heart. A friend I knew from high school came by and told me he had "become a Christian." He invited me to attend classes with him at Philadelphia College of the Bible, where I drank in everything I was taught with hungry joy and anticipation. At night, Ralph and I would go listen to a speaker or simply hang out at a diner talking about God, life, girls, and the abundant living we were sure was ahead. That fall, I went to a retreat in the mountains of Pennsylvania and met a longhaired girl whose heart God had recently courted and won. We sat for hours, talking about our personal longings and fears. We even prayed out loud together, a totally new concept to me.

"Becoming a Christian," however, doesn't necessarily solve the dilemma of the arrows, as I was soon to realize. Mine were still lodged deep and refused to allow some angry wound inside to heal. My resulting ambivalence colored every thought, action, and relationship of those important years. One day, at my by-then fiancée's request, I sat for five hours on the shore of a lake trying to understand the doubts I had about getting married. I knew no more at the end of the day than I did at the beginning. I had no one, at that point in my life, to help me understand the ambivalence created by the Message of the Arrows. No one who could fit the contradictory messages of the two revelations (the Romance and the Arrows) into any kind of story that would allow for life's unknowns even as my heart stayed open to the intimacy of Romance. So I became my own author and killed the one to control the other. I broke my engagement. I gave up the mystery of the Romance for a story that was much more predictable—which is to say, aloneness.

I allowed the romance to revive with another girl, Ginny, who eventually became my wife, when I was twenty-eight, but the arrows refused to be silent and I lived my late twenties and early thirties in a continuing blind reaction to the two revelations that vied for my soul. An old and familiar feeling began to make itself known from somewhere in the vicinity of my heart; a loneliness, an emptiness, a kind of ache and longing for something and someone I couldn't quite define. Feeling agitated and betrayed by such adulterous feelings, I pushed them down and threw myself even more intensely into Christian involvement and service. I began teaching our church's college-and-career class, became the singles pastor, and worked with our high school kids. Ginny and I were both teachers and used our summers to go to the mission fields in Mexico and the Dominican Republic as summer assistants with Wycliffe Bible Translators and Teen Missions. I even attended those strange Christian phenomena known as "potluck suppers" in the church activity hall.

These were all good things, but there was a part of me that refused to be healed, or filled, or freed, or whatever it was that my heart refused to be silent about. And since I never bothered to ask myself many questions (at least not the right questions) about what I felt or believed, I lived those years in a tangled web of fantasy divorced from present living and reality motivated by agnosticism and resignation. I lived in reaction to a series of happenings and circumstances that I felt unable to understand or even use as a way of understanding. I lived in the place where Forrest Gump found himself as he stood at the grave of his lifelong love, Jenny. "I don't know if we each have a destiny, or if we're all just floating around accident-like, on the breeze."

Many of you reading my story can relate to an inner journey that *feels* something like my own, even though the scenes of your outer story may be very different. The sense of being part of some bigger story, a purposeful adventure that is the Christian life, begins to drain away again after those first-love years in spite of everything we can do to stop it. Instead of a love affair with God, your life begins to feel more like a series of repetitive behaviors, like reading the same chapter of a book or writing the same novel over and over. The orthodoxy we try to live out, defined as "Believe and Behave Accordingly" is not a sufficient story line to satisfy whatever turmoil and longing our heart is trying to tell us about. Somehow our head and heart are on separate journeys and neither feels like life.

Eventually this division of head and heart culminates in one of two directions. We can either deaden our heart or divide our life into two parts, where our outer story becomes the theater of the should and our inner story the theater of needs, the place where we quench the thirst of our heart with whatever water is available. I chose the second route, living what I thought of as my religious life with increasing dryness and cynicism while I found "water" where I could: in sexual fantasies, alcohol, the next dinner out, late-night violence videos, gaining more knowledge through religious seminars—whatever would slake the thirsty restlessness inside. Whichever path we choose—heart deadness or heart and head separation—the Arrows win and we lose heart.

This is the story of all our lives, in one way or another. The haunting of the Romance and the Message of the Arrows are so radically different and they seem so mutually exclusive they split our hearts in two. In every way that the Romance is full of beauty and wonder, the Arrows are equally powerful in their ugliness and devastation. The Romance seems to promise a life of wholeness through a deep connection with the great Heart behind the universe. The Arrows deny it, telling us, "You are on your own. There is no Romance, no one strong and kind who is calling you to an exotic adventure." The Romance says, "This world is a benevolent place." The Arrows mock such naïveté, warning us, "Just watch yourself—disaster is a moment away." The Romance invites us to trust. The Arrows intimidate us into self-reliance.

It is as if we have all been "set up" for a loss of heart. I think about two couples who chose to go through marriage counseling with me, not because their relationships were terrible but because both couples desired to live before God and each other with more freedom and love. Hannah and Mike (not their real names) were in their early twenties and had been married just a few months. Hannah had a difficult life before her marriage, moving from town to town with no relationship with her real father. Mike was a loner before he met Hannah, nursing the wounds from his own Arrows in solitude. Hannah and Mike both loved the outdoors and as their love for each other grew, they looked forward to a long life in the mountains with their yet-to-be-born children. One year after their marriage, I spoke at Hannah's memorial service in the Garden of the Gods. Cancer took her life almost before she had a chance to fight it.

Sam and Leslie (not their real names) came for counseling after long years of fruitful service for God on the mission field. They were still young, in their early fifties, and they knew there were some unhealed things between them that would prevent them from having the deeper intimacy they both longed for in the years ahead. They entered into looking at their marriage with courage and hope at a time in life when it would have been easy to just stay with the status quo. They looked forward to enjoying the time to come with their children and grandchildren as well as a deeper intimacy with each other. Not long ago I stood at Leslie's graveside as Sam and the children said good-bye to her, Leslie also having been struck down by cancer.

What are Mike and Sam left to conclude? Mike opened his heart only to lose everything in exactly the way he feared. Sam hoped to live out his years with Leslie, enjoying his family and the fruits of all his years of service, only to face the years ahead alone. The Arrows strike at the most vital places in our hearts, the things we care most about. The deepest questions we ever ask are directly related to our heart's greatest needs and the answers life gives us shape our images of ourselves, of life, and of God. *Who am I?* The Romance whispers that we are someone special, that our heart is good because it is made for someone good; the Arrows tell us we are a dime a dozen, worthless, even dark and twisted, dirty. *Where is life to be found?* The Romance tells us life will flourish when we give it away in love and heroic sacrifice. The Arrows tell us that we must arrange for what little life there may be, manipulating our world and all the while watching our backs. "God is good," the Romance tells us. "You can release the well-being of your heart to him." The Arrows strike back, "Don't ever let life out of your control," and they seem to impale with such authority, unlike the gentle urges of the Romance, that in the end we are driven to find some way to contain them. The only way seems to be to kill our longing for the Romance, much in the same way we harden our heart to someone who hurts us. *If I don't want so much*, we believe, *I won't be so vulnerable*. Instead of dealing with the Arrows, we silence the longing. That seems to be our only hope. And so we lose heart.

Which is the truer message? If we try to hang on to the Romance, what are we to do with our wounds and the awful tragedies of life? How can we keep our heart alive in the face of such deadly Arrows? Is it possible for Mike to risk opening his heart to love again? Can Sam ever totally trust the God he served for so long? How many losses can a heart take? If we deny the wounds or try to minimize them, we deny a part of our heart and end up living a shallow optimism that frequently becomes a demand that the world be better than it is. On the other hand, if we embrace the Arrows as the final word on life, we despair, which is another way to lose heart. To lose hope has the same effect on our heart as it would be to stop breathing. If only there were someone to help us reconcile our deepest longings with our greatest fears.

In my thirties, I didn't know that the One who answered the "religious prayer" of my mid-twenties ("God, help me, because I am lost") was the same One who wooed me so long ago in the magic of the singers and even in the harsh coldness of that November day. If I had known, the years of my religiosity would have been filled with much more joy and confusion, mourning and hope, patience and spontaneity, and conviction and uncareful love than they have been. I would have lived with a confidence that the Arrows aren't the final word. But I had lost my own story with the loss of my family as a boy, and along with it any sense of a larger story that would reconcile the two messages my heart had known.

4

A Story Big Enough to Live In

Romance is the deepest thing in life, romance is deeper even than reality.

G. K. Chesterton

Is THERE a reality that corresponds to the deepest desires of our heart? Who gets the last word—the Romance or the Arrows? We need to know, so we are constantly, every moment of our lives, trying to make sense out of our experiences. We look for coherence, a flow, an assurance that things fit together. We want, we *need* to reconcile the two revelations Brent has been describing. Our problem is most of us live our lives like a movie we've arrived at twenty minutes late. The action is well under way and we haven't a clue what's happening. Who are these people? Who are the good guys and who are the bad guys? Why are they doing that? What's going on? We sense that something really important, perhaps even glorious, is taking place, and yet it all seems so *random*. Beauty catches us by surprise and makes us wish for more, but then the Arrows come and we are pierced. As Chesterton wrote,

> We all feel the riddle of the earth without anyone to point it out. The mystery of life is the plainest part of it. . . . Every stone or flower is a hieroglyphic of which we have lost the key; with every step of our lives we enter into the middle of some story which we are certain to misunderstand. (*Orthodoxy*)

No wonder it's so hard to live from our heart! We find ourselves in the middle of a story that is sometimes wonderful,
sometimes awful, often a confusing mixture of both, and we
haven't the slightest clue how to make sense of it all. Worse, we
try to interpret the meaning of life with only fragments, isolated
incidents, feelings, and images without reference to the story of
which these scenes are merely a part. It can't be done, because,
as Julia Gatta pointed out, "Experience, no matter how accurately understood, can never furnish its own interpretation." So
we look for someone to interpret life for us. Our interpreters
will usually be the primary people in our lives when we are
young, our parents or grandparents or another key figure. They
shape our understanding of the story in which we find ourselves
and tell us what to do with the Romance, the Arrows, and our
hearts.

Brent was often left without an interpreter as fathers came
and went. I (John) was more fortunate; I had a grandfather who
stepped into my life at the very moment the Arrows were about
to take over, during the years my father was engulfed in the sinister battle we call alcoholism. Trained as a civil engineer, my
father fell into a career in sales just when the U.S. Army glutted
the market with engineers after World War II. Arthur Miller
captured the tenuous nature of his life in *Death of a Salesman*:
"He's a man way out there in the blue, riding on a smile and a
shoeshine. And when they start not smiling back—that's an
earthquake. And then you get yourself a couple of spots on your
hat, and you're finished. Nobody dast blame this man." My
mother went back to college and then to work to help make
ends meet, and I was largely left on my own to form my understanding of the story of life and my role in it.

My grandfather, "Pop," filled an empty place in my soul at
that critical moment. He was my hero, a cowboy and a gentle-
man in a Stetson and boots. Spending summers on his ranch was
a schoolboy's dream—riding horses, chasing frogs, harassing the

big old cows when I was sure no one was looking. I remember riding in his old Ford pickup, Pop with his cowboy hat and leather work gloves, waving at nearly everyone on the road. Folks seemed to wave back with a sense of respect. It gave me a settled feeling that someone was in charge, someone strong and loving.

Pop loved me as a boy and called me to be a man. He taught me to saddle and ride a horse—not merely for fun, but to take my place on a working ranch. Together we explored the open spaces of the eastern Oregon sagebrush, mending fences, tending sick cattle, fishing Huck Finn–style with willow branches and a piece of string. Early in the morning we'd go for coffee, milk, and doughnuts down at the diner where everyone knew us by name. Sunday afternoons we'd go "visiting"—calling on relatives in nearby towns and farms. Together they would sit and chat, telling family stories that gave me a sense of being part of something larger than myself. Even though my own world was shaken by the earthquake of my father's struggle, I knew there was another world where things were well and I could have a place in it.

During my teenage years visits to the ranch grew fewer and farther between. My father, fighting his own battles, was unable to teach me how to fight mine. Screaming to know someone was there for me, I tried nearly every protest available to unsupervised teens in American culture. At fifteen I was arrested for breaking and entering. I can't even remember what my parents said or did; perhaps I had already broken their hearts as only a prodigal son can. But hours later I found myself free to roam again. On the surface, I was relieved to escape punishment; far deeper, in the place in our heart where the story forms, the disappointment was more than I could bear. Why didn't they *do* something? I knew what I'd done was wrong; why wouldn't somebody show me the right way? It was a major Arrow. The message instructed me in the deep terror that there was no one strong enough to care for my soul, to pick me up and set me straight when I'd fallen. I was alone.

I was seventeen when I last saw my grandfather. The brain cancer that eventually killed him had already taken a loathsome toll. The man who had always stood larger than life was stooped and withered. His ranch, a picture of his life, was failing. I simply had no context for it, nothing larger to give it redemptive meaning. So I distanced myself from him and from the final piece of evidence that I was on my own in the world. When he died, I couldn't bring myself to attend the funeral.

Years later, in the summer of 1993, I stood by my grandfather's grave for the first time. After sixteen years I had made a pilgrimage to face the reality I had so long run from. It lay there in quiet, undeniable triumph: the Message of the Arrows.

Whether we feel it with the finality that Brent and I did, or as a lingering fear in the corner of our minds, most of us sense that we are alone in the world. No one has ever been there for us with the strength, tenderness, and consistency that we long for. Even in the best situations, people eventually let us down. Our personal drama leaves us little hope for an Author who is taking the story toward a good conclusion. Chesterton said we're certain to misunderstand the story we find ourselves in and he was right. Furthermore, those closest to us often help in the misinterpretation.

Still, we must make some sense of things. Life goes on and so must we. In order to participate or merely survive, we will find some story to live in.

Why Story?

The deepest convictions of our heart are formed by stories and reside there in the images and emotions of story. As a young boy, around the time my heart began to suspect that the world was a fearful place and I was on my own to find my way through it, I read the story of a Scottish discus thrower from the nineteenth century. He lived in the days before professional trainers and developed his skills alone, in the highlands of his native village. He even made his own iron discus from the description he read in a book. What he did not know was that the discus used in competition was made of wood with an *outer rim* of iron. His was solid metal and weighed three or four times as much as those being used by his would-be challengers. This committed Scotsman marked out in his field the distance of the current record throw and trained day and night to be able to match it. For nearly a year, he labored under the self-imposed burden of the extra weight. But he became very, very good. He reached the point at which he could throw his iron discus the record distance, maybe farther. He was ready.

My Scotsman (I had begun to closely identify with him) traveled south to England for his first competition. When he arrived at the games, he was handed the official wooden discus—which he promptly threw like a tea saucer. He set a new record, a distance so far beyond those of his competitors that no one could touch him. He thus remained the uncontested champion for many years.

Something in my heart connected with this story. *So, that's how you do it: Train under a great burden and you will be so far beyond the rest of the world you will be untouchable*. It became a defining image for my life, formed in and from a story.

Life is not a list of propositions, it is a series of dramatic scenes. As Eugene Peterson said, "We live in narrative, we live in story. Existence has a story shape to it. We have a beginning and an end, we have a plot, we have characters." Story is the language of the heart. Our souls speak not in the naked facts of mathematics or the abstract propositions of systematic theology; they speak the images and emotions of story. Contrast your enthusiasm for studying a textbook with the offer to go to a movie, read a novel, or listen to the stories of someone else's life. Elie Wiesel suggests that "God created man because he loves stories." So if we're going to find the answer to the riddle of the earth—and of our own existence—we'll find it in story.

Once upon a time the Western world had a story. Imagine you lived in the High Middle Ages. Your world was permeated with Christian imagery. You marked the days by the sound of church bells and the weeks and months according to the liturgical calendar. You lived in *anno domini*, the year of our Lord. It wasn't football season, it was Advent. Your role models were the saints, whose feast days were regular reminders of a drama greater than yourself. The architecture of the cathedral, the music, literature, and sculpture all gave you a vision of transcendence, reminding you of the central elements of that great story. Even the everyday language reflected the Christian understanding of life's story, expressions like "God be with you," "upon my soul," and "by Christ's blood." Birth and death, love and loss—all of your personal experiences would be shaped and interpreted by that larger story.

But you don't live in the Middle Ages, you live in the Postmodern Era. For hundreds of years, our culture has been losing its story. The Enlightenment dismissed the idea that there is an Author but tried to hang on to the idea that we could still have a larger story, life could still make sense, and everything was headed in a good direction. Western culture rejected the mystery and transcendence of the Middle Ages and placed its confidence in pragmatism and progress, the pillars of the Modern Era, the Age of Reason. But once we had rid ourselves of the Author, it didn't take long to lose the larger story. In the Postmodern Era, all we have left is our small stories. It's not pentecost, it's time for spring training. Our role models are movie stars, and the biggest taste of transcendence is the opening of the ski season. Our best expressions are on the level of "Have a nice day." The only reminder we have of a story beyond our own is the evening news, an arbitrary collection of scenes and images without any bigger picture into which they fit. The central belief of our times is that there is no story, nothing hangs together, all we have are bits and pieces, the random days of our lives. Tragedy still brings us to tears and heroism still lifts our hearts, but there is no context for any of it. Life is just a sequence of images and emotions without rhyme or reason.

So, what are we left to do? Create our own story line to bring some meaning to our experiences. Our heart is made to live in a larger story; having lost that we do the best we can by developing our own smaller dramas.

Look at the things people get caught up in: sports, politics, soap operas, rock bands. Desperate for something larger to give our lives transcendence, we try to lose ourselves in the smallest kinds of stories. Some of us choose the "Why does everything go wrong for me?" story. The plot of life is a tragedy, and we are playing the role of the victim of cruel circumstances. Our Arrows are our identity. This is an immensely popular story line because it relieves us of having to take any real responsibility for our lives. Victims demand to be understood, but don't you dare require anything of them.

And then there is the survivor, living in a life where the plot is a siege. The world is a dangerous and unpredictable place, so I will hunker down and survive, taking little risk, doing what I can to protect myself even if it means cutting myself off from others and from my own dreams. These stories focus on the Arrows at the expense of the Romance.

On the other hand, some of us are trying to live out a story line that preserves the Romance in some way. Though it takes a lot of energy to push the mess of life out of sight in order to maintain the belief that mystery and magic are the final word, we try. The most popular option is romantic love, the idea that somewhere out there is that special someone who will sweep you off your feet, take your breath away, with whom life would be one idyllic adventure and sex an unending ecstasy. It is the theme of popular music, the false transcendence of our day. Women especially are attracted to this story line; witness the success of novelist Danielle Steel and her imitators. The divorce rate ought to be proof enough of the failure of this story. It's not so much that lovers cannot live with each other as that they cannot live without the Haunting, which they mistook for romantic love. So they move to the next partner, trying to capture that evasive feeling again.

The leading false transcendence among men is the sports story. Men either pursue their longings for adventure through their own recreational activities or they lose themselves vicariously in their favorite players and teams, or in their children's sports. Business also fits into the story of life as a Big Game. *Sure, things are unpredictable, but some people seem to win and I'm determined to be one of them. I'll stay on top, travel light, and move fast.* We identify with a sports team or a company because we are allowed to belong to something bigger than our small worlds. Our heroes are the few winners, of course, while the losers are quickly pushed out of the camera's view.

Christians can opt for one of these, or choose a more "spiritual" version. The Religious Man or Woman is a popular story option in which we try to reduce the wildness of life by constructing a system of promises and rewards, a contract that will obligate God to grant us exemption from the Arrows. It really doesn't matter what the particular group bargain is—doctrinal adherence, moral living, or some sort of spiritual experience— the desire is the same: taming God in order to tame life. Never mind those deep yearnings of the soul; never mind the nagging awareness that God is not cooperating. If the system isn't working, it's because we're not doing it right. There's always something to work on, with the promise of abundant life just around the corner. Plenty of churches and leaders are ready to show you how to cut a deal.

All these stories comprise what James McClendon calls the

"tournament of narratives" in our culture, a clash of many small dramas competing for our heart. Through baseball and politics and music and sex and even church, we are searching desperately for a larger story in which to live and find our role. All of these smaller stories offer a taste of meaning, adventure, or connectedness. But none of them offer the real thing; they aren't large enough. Our loss of confidence in a larger story is the reason we demand immediate gratification. We need a sense of being alive now, for now is all we have. Without a past that was planned for us and a future that waits for us, we are trapped in the present. There's not enough room for our souls in the present.

Our attempts to construct a story to live in eventually fail because, as Robert Jenson has said, "Human consciousness is too obscure a mystery to itself for us to script our own lives." Inevitably, we leave significant parts of our souls out of the story. If our particular version fails to take both of life's messages into account, to grant them proper weight, it will destroy us. Denying the tragedy of life requires such effort that it tears the soul apart. Believing that in the end there is only tragedy kills the most tender, "alive" parts of us. Trapped in an eternal present, we come to a sickness of heart like that of Shakespeare's Macbeth, the Scottish nobleman who sells his soul to play the role of king in his own small story. At the end of his life he laments,

> I am sick at heart. . . .
> To-morrow, and to-morrow, and to-morrow,
> Creeps in this petty pace from day to day
> To the last syllable of recorded time;
> Life's but a walking shadow, a poor player
> That struts and frets his hour upon the stage
> And then is heard no more. It is a tale
> Told by an idiot, full of sound and fury,
> Signifying nothing. (*Act V, Scene V*)

The Sacred Romance

There *is* another way, one that grants the "devil his due" in all the tragedy of life, but that also keeps hope alive that the haunting of the Romance is no illusion, either. Children aren't a bad place to look when we're trying to get beyond the cynicism of adulthood and so it shouldn't surprise us that most children have found a way of reconciling the messages. Before skepticism takes over (what we mistakenly call maturity), children intuit the true Story as a fairy tale. If you'll remember, the best fairy tales aren't romantic in the poor sense of the word. They are realistic, only more so. There are ogres and evil sorcerers and wicked stepmothers, to be sure. But they are neither the whole story nor even the heart of it. There are genuine heroes and heroines and a cause to live for that is worth dying for. There is a quest or a journey strewn with danger and the stakes could never be higher.

My boys are at the age when cowboys are among their greatest heroes. Our days are often filled with gunfights and stories of daring adventure. Several nights ago, as I was tucking seven-year-old Samuel into bed, we began talking about the future. I asked him what he wanted to do when he grows up. With a grave severity in his eye he looked at me and said, "I'm going to bring back the West." His heart knew that he was made for noble things. Our heart knows it, too, if we will let it speak to us.

Now, what is intriguing is that this metaphor is the closest one to the way in which the Scriptures present the gospel—as a Sacred Romance. If that surprises you then it is good news, for any explanation bold enough to encompass the meaning of life ought to have at least two elements: It ought to be weighty enough to sustain both messages and it ought to come as a bit of a surprise. We have lived for so long with a "propositional" approach to Christianity we have nearly lost its true meaning. As Mary Stewart Van Leeuwen says,

Much of it hinges on your view of scripture. Are you playing proof-text poker with Genesis plus the Gospels and Paul's epistles, with everything else just sort of a big mystery in between—except maybe Psalms and Proverbs, which you use devotionally? Or do you see scripture as being a cosmic drama—creation, fall, redemption, future hope—dramatic narratives that you can apply to all areas of life? (*Prism* interview)

For centuries prior to our Modern Era, the church viewed the gospel as a Romance, a cosmic drama whose themes permeated our own stories and drew together all the random scenes in a redemptive wholeness. But our rationalistic approach to life, which has dominated Western culture for hundreds of years, has stripped us of that, leaving a faith that is barely more than mere fact-telling. Modern evangelicalism reads like an IRS 1040 form: It's true, all the data is there, but it doesn't take your breath away. As British theologian Alister McGrath warns, the Bible is not primarily a doctrinal sourcebook: "To reduce revelation to principles or concepts is to suppress the element of mystery, holiness and wonder to God's self-disclosure. 'First principles' may enlighten and inform; they do not force us to our knees in reverence and awe, as with Moses at the burning bush, or the disciples in the presence of the risen Christ" (*A Passion for Truth*).

Could it be that our lives actually make sense, every part—the good and the bad? Those deep yearnings that catch us by surprise when we hear a certain song on the radio, or watch our children when they aren't aware of being watched, are telling us something that *is* truer about life than the Message of the Arrows. It seems too good to be true, which ought to raise even deeper suspicions that it is true. As Chesterton recounts in *Orthodoxy*, he "had always believed that the world involved magic: now I thought that perhaps it involved a magician. . . . I had always felt life first as a story; and if there is a story there is a storyteller."

According to the part of the story God has allowed us to see, the Haunting we sense is his calling us forth on a journey. The resurrection of our heart requires that the Sacred Romance be true and that is precisely what the Scriptures tell us. As Frederick Buechner reminds us in his wonderful book *Telling the Truth: The Gospel as Tragedy, Comedy and Fairy Tale*, the world of the gospel *is* the world of fairy tale, with one notable exception:

> It is a world of magic and mystery, of deep darkness and flickering starlight. It is a world where terrible things happen and wonderful things too. It is a world where goodness is pitted against evil, love against hate, order against chaos, in a great struggle where often it is hard to be sure who belongs to which side because appearances are endlessly deceptive. Yet for all its confusion and wildness, it is a world where the battle goes ultimately to the good, who live happily ever after, and where in the long run everybody, good and evil alike, becomes known by his true name. . . . That is the fairy tale of the Gospel with, of course, one crucial difference from all other fairy tales, which is that the claim made for it is that it is true, that it not only happened once upon a time but has kept on happening ever since and is happening still.

Let us explore together the drama that God has been weaving since before the beginning of time, which he has also placed in our heart. Who are the main players in this larger story? What is the plot? How do we fit in? As we rediscover the oldest story in the world, one that is forever young, we journey into the heart of God and toward the recovery of our own hearts. For perhaps God would be reason enough to stay open to the Romance if we knew he would keep us safe. And therein we experience a great fear and confusion.

5

The Wildness of God

[We live our lives before] the wild, dangerous,
unfettered and free character of the living God.
Walter Bruggeman

THE UNKNOWN Romancing or the Message of the Arrows—which captures the essence of life? Should we keep our hearts open to the Romance or concentrate on protecting ourselves from the Arrows? Should we live with hopeful abandon, trusting in a larger story whose ending is good or should we live in our small stories and glean what we can from the Romance while trying to avoid the Arrows?

Perhaps God, as the Author of the story we're all living in, would tilt the scale in a favorable direction if we knew we could trust him. And therein lies our dilemma. There seems to be no direct correlation between the way we live our lives and the resulting fate God has in store for us, at least on this earth. Abraham's grandson, Jacob, lives the life of a manipulator and is blessed. Jesus lives for the sake of others and is crucified. And we never quite know when we're going to run into the uncertainty of the part God has written for us in his play, whether our character has significant lines yet to speak or will even survive the afternoon.

I (Brent) was confronted with my own questions about him at the most elemental level when I was a fourth grader in David C. Crockett elementary school in Bryan, Texas. As a Northerner recently moved from New Jersey, I quickly discovered that there had been a Civil War and there were still amends to be made. That fall, for what seemed like weeks, the four of us from Northern states were sent to one end of the playground where we waited to be attacked by the forces of the Confederacy. And since we were considerably outnumbered, unlike those 1860s Union infantry, we were soon enough "captured" and taken to prison camp. This camp was a large mulch pile of dead leaves surrounded by chicken wire and presided over by a sixth grader named Jimmy. Jimmy's favorite form of punishment was to drag the terrified waif last captured to the middle of the pile and lower his considerable 150-pound bulk until the prisoner disappeared from view. I cannot describe the terror I felt at being taken to Jimmy. Much of any leg speed I have came from a determination to be the last one captured on a given day, in hopes that the school bell would ring before my interment.

I remember one of my friends, a boy from Ohio named Terry, being sat on so long one day that I feared he was dead. I looked around for teachers or parents or even sympathetic sixth graders who would help us. No one came. I finally yelled for Jimmy to let Terry up before he killed him. With a smile, and in best bad guy form from the movies, he rose majestically and ordered my guards to put me in Terry's place.

I remember landing in the leaves with only the thought I'd be suffocated, or worse, made to cry in front of everybody. Before Jimmy could lower himself all the way, I squirmed free, jumped the chicken wire, and raced to the far ends of the playground to outlast the recess bell. Somehow I could never find the way to express this daily terror to my parents. I felt totally alone with it.

The Question in Our Heart

Of course, all of us have lived through events such as I have described, some much, much worse and, if they took place in the setting of family, school, or work, perhaps lasting for years. The terror we enter and the seeming lack of rescue from it leave us with a deeply imprinted question about God that we hide in our heart, sometimes not allowing the light of day to touch it for years, even deep into our spiritual journey. We cover the question with rationalizations that let him off the hook and allow us to still believe, but our beliefs rest on foundations that move and quake under us. It is easy to reason that Jimmy and those sixth graders were just bad; you know, "not raised in very good homes." And of course, our rationalizations do bear a modicum of truth that keeps us from dealing with the question lodged deep in our heart, hidden from our conscious mind: "Do you care for me, God?"

What's under that question?

Blaise Pascal, in his *Pensees,* says, "The heart has its reasons that reason knows not of." What's under that question is our personal stories, often punctuated by the Message of the Arrows: parents who were emotionally absent; bedtimes without words or hugs; ears that were too big and noses that were too small; others chosen for playground games while we were not; and prayers about all these things seemingly met with silence. And embedded in our stories, deep down in our heart, in a place so well guarded that they have rarely if ever been exposed to the light of day, are other grief-laden and often angry questions: "God, why did you allow this to happen to me? Why did you make me like this? What will you allow to happen next?" In the secret places of our heart, we believe God is the One who did not protect us from these things or even the One who perpetrated them upon us. Our questions about him make us begin to live with a deep apprehension that clings anxiously to the depths of our hearts. . . . "Do you really care for me, God?"

This is the question that has shipwrecked many of our hearts, leaving them grounded on reefs of pain and doubt, no longer free to accompany us on spiritual pilgrimage. We might be able to rationalize away that question by telling ourselves that we need to be more careful, or that sometimes others are just bad. We can even breathe a sigh of relief when we realize that trouble has come from our own sin. But even the careful, legalistic, and constricted lifestyle that arises out of thinking we can avoid trouble through our own devices shipwrecks when the Arrows seem to strike us out of nowhere. What are we to make of God's wildness in allowing these things to happen?

A Part Too Large

Indeed, the things that have happened to us often suggest that the real script of the play we're all living in is "God is indifferent" rather than "God is love." Deep down in our heart, in the place where the story is formed, this experience of God as indifferent drives us to write our own scripts, as John described in Chapter 4. Job apparently lived with this anxiety about God even before his tribulations descended upon him, as evidenced by his exclamation from the ashes of his home and his life: "What I *feared* has come upon me; what I *dreaded* has happened to me" (Job 3:25).

Job was a God-fearing man and yet something in him suspected that faith in God did not necessarily translate into peace and safety. Of course, Job had no inkling of the discussion going on in heaven between God and Satan. It was a debate over whether the foundation of God's kingdom was based on genuine love or power. And astonishingly, God was placing the perception of his own integrity as well as the reputation of his whole kingdom on the genuineness of Job's heart. Eavesdrop with me on one of the most revealing conversations in the Scriptures:

> One day the angels came to present themselves before the LORD, and Satan also came with them. The LORD said to Satan, "Where have you come from?"

Satan answered the LORD, "From roaming through the earth and going back and forth in it."

Then the LORD said to Satan, "Have you considered my servant Job? There is no one on earth like him; he is blameless and upright, a man who fears God and shuns evil."

"Does Job fear God for nothing?" Satan replied. "Have you not put a hedge around him and his household and everything he has? You have blessed the work of his hands, so that his flocks and herds are spread throughout the land. But stretch out your hand and strike everything he has, and he will surely curse you to your face."

The LORD said to Satan, "Very well, then, everything he has is in your hands, but on the man himself do not lay a finger." . . .

On another day the angels came to present themselves before the LORD, and Satan also came with them to present himself before him. And the LORD said to Satan, "Where have you come from?"

Satan answered the LORD, "From roaming through the earth and going back and forth in it."

Then the LORD said to Satan, "Have you considered my servant Job? There is no one on earth like him; he is blameless and upright, a man who fears God and shuns evil. And he still maintains his integrity, though you incited me against him to ruin him without any reason."

"Skin for skin!" Satan replied. "A man will give all he has for his own life. But stretch out your hand and strike his flesh and bones, and he will surely curse you to your face."

The LORD said to Satan, "Very well, then, he is in your hands; but you must spare his life."

So Satan went out from the presence of the LORD and afflicted Job with painful sores from the soles of his feet to the top of his head. Then Job took a piece of broken pottery and scraped himself with it as he sat among the ashes.

His wife said to him, "Are you still holding on to your integrity? Curse God and die!"

He replied, "You are talking like a foolish woman. Shall we accept good from God, and not trouble?"

In all this, Job did not sin in what he said. *(Job 1:6–12; 2:1–10)*

When Job's three friends came along and witnessed the devastation of his life, they tore their clothes, sprinkled dust on their heads, and appropriately, sat in silence with him for seven days because they saw how great his suffering was. The story doesn't tell us much about what they were feeling during those seven days, but their subsequent counsel gives us a pretty good idea of what they were thinking. Eliphaz the Temanite basically responded to Job's continued groanings by saying, "Job, you've been our man. We've watched you carefully to see how you gain God's blessings so that we can do it just like you do. You know how this religion business works. If you're innocent, you'll be okay. If you've sinned, you won't. Since you're not okay, you've obviously blown it. There can be no other explanation for what's going on here" (Job 4:1–8).

God's direct correction of Job's friends exposed the secret demand of their hearts. They, like all of us do at one time or another, had been relating to God like one of the Mesopotamian household gods that the peoples in the Middle East were so familiar with.

The cultures in the cradle of civilization lived with a pantheon of gods who themselves existed in a kind of hierarchy. There were gods of war, fertility, and harvest who were acknowledged by the culture as a whole, and under these, a litany of household gods, usually statues made of crafted wood, clay, and precious metals, that were placed on the family mantel. People related to each of these gods by means of specific rituals and ceremonies whereby their protection and favor could be gained. Each family literally "owned" their own god.

To use an illustration from our culture, these household gods were somewhat like having a mobster for a neighbor. To those outside the neighborhood, the mobster may seem fearful and somewhat sinister. But if you're his immediate neighbor and treat him with deference and respect, he may get you a good deal on aluminum siding or a new car. Or he might have a bag of dead cats deposited on the doorstep of the man down the street, who, you casually mentioned, was allowing his dog to dig in your flower beds.

When the living God of the Old Testament came along, he seemed to fit right in with this way of thinking, describing himself as the God of Abraham, Isaac, and Jacob. He gave Moses a regimen of laws, rituals, and ceremonies to be followed if the Israelites were to gain his favor. Everything should have worked out fine. The familiar household-god religion was very simple and well understood by everyone: Simply obey the prescribed rules, regulations, and rituals that the god thought were important, for whatever reason, and he would be appeased and give his blessing. The Israelites never bothered to read between the lines. They were totally unprepared and unwilling to consider the thought that they, like Job, were involved in a much bigger drama.

Indeed, when we consider how central a part Job was given in the drama God was directing, we are confronted with the reality that we, too, could be in the same position. It seems that the part God has written for us is much too big and certainly too dangerous. Paul confirms this thought in Ephesians when he tells us, "The church, you see, is not peripheral to the world; the world is peripheral to the church. The church is Christ's body, in which he speaks and acts, by which he fills everything with his presence" (1:22–23, *The Message*). Every human being is of great significance to God, but those whom God has drawn to believe in him are center stage in a drama of cosmic proportions.

When we look at Job's time on center stage, we find that God not only allows the Prince of Darkness to come before his throne, he points Job out to him and, in effect, unleashes him on the defenseless man. This is very much akin to a policeman drawing the attention of a gang of thugs to a young man walking lawfully along the street with his wife, children, and belongings. He then gives the gangsters permission to test the man's respect for the law by mugging and robbing him, and killing his children. I find myself asking, "Was this really necessary to test Job's heart? What's going on here anyway?" I want to ask, "If God is the author, producer, and director of this play, *what kind of a story is he telling?*"

I am filled with not a little outrage as well as an anxiety that wants to ask for a much smaller part in the play than Job had; or possibly even a role in a more off-Broadway production that I could help direct. You know, something like *God Helps Brent Pursue Money, Wealth, and Fame While Living a Quiet Life*. There is something frightening about being in a play in which the director may allow the plot to descend on my character from a totally unknown direction, a direction that may cause me deep emotional or even physical harm. It is something like having the stage lights dropped from high overhead during one of my scenes without telling me, leaving me no chance to change my mark before they fall.

God's artistry as Playwright of the story we find ourselves living in often seems to use up characters like trailer courts in tornado season. He assures us, notably in the Psalms, that he sees our pain and cares for us, and that our tormentors will be judged, but he still calls us firmly to our marks, regardless of disease, calamity, age, sex, or strength.

He comes to Job in the midst of his loss, pain, and indeed the nearness of death and says, referring to the ongoing discussion between Job and his friends,

> "Who is this that darkens my counsel
> with words without knowledge?
> Brace yourself like a man;
> I will question you,
> and you shall answer me" *(Job 38:2–3)*.

This is followed by his lengthy interrogation of Job's understanding of even the physical creation, much less any more profound issues. I must admit there is something in me as a man that feels strangely respected by this approach while another part of me thinks, *How unfeeling and cold.*

When God comes to call Jeremiah to be his prophet of hard sayings to Judah, Jeremiah protests, saying, "'Ah, Sovereign LORD . . . I do not know how to speak; I am only a child.' But the LORD said to me, 'Do not say, "I am only a child." You must go to everyone I send you to and say whatever I command you. Do not be afraid of them, for I am with you and will rescue you,' declares the LORD" (Jer. 1:6–8).

God is saying that these things will be done through Jeremiah's dependence on his strength and provision, and that he will rescue him. Yet there is something about God's rescues that make them a little less timely than dialing 911. He leaves Abraham with his knife raised and ready to plunge into Isaac's heart, and Isaac waiting for the knife to descend; he leaves Joseph languishing for years in an Egyptian prison; he allows the Israelites to suffer four hundred years of bondage under the Egyptians and leaves those same Israelites backed against the Red Sea with Pharaoh's chariots thundering down on them. He abandons Jesus to the cross and does not rescue him at all. And then there are those of us who, along with the saints under heaven's very altar, are groaning under the weight of things gone wrong, waiting for that same Jesus to return and sweep us up with him in power and glory. "How long, O Lord?" we whisper in our weariness and pain.

Indeed, God calls us to battles where the deck appears stacked in favor of those who are his enemies and ours, just to increase the drama of the play. And there is the clear picture, even from God himself, that he does so to enhance his own glory.

In C. S. Lewis's novel *The Lion, the Witch, and the Wardrobe,* of The Chronicles of Narnia series, four children, Peter, Susan, Edmund, and Lucy, pass through the wardrobe's portal to find the kingdom of Narnia imprisoned under the spell of the White Witch. Aslan the lion, who is the king of Narnia, is nowhere to be found. Although rumor has it "He is on the move," he appears to have abandoned his kingdom to the White Witch, who spends her leisure time turning the inhabitants into lawn statuary.

The four children set out to explore this strange and somewhat frightening new country that is locked under evil's spell. They come upon Mr. and Mrs. Beaver, a husband and wife still faithful to Aslan. The Beavers assure the children that Aslan is about to return to set things right and that prophecy suggests that they have a very important, even central part to play in the drama about to unfold. Indeed, they learn they are to actually rule with Aslan from Cair Paravel itself, Aslan's royal city.

Faced with all this fearful yet exciting news, Lucy and Susan's thoughts go to what Aslan is actually like. If he is a king who is safe, they reason, that will certainly be of great comfort in light of the battle being all but lost.

"Is—is he a man?" asked Lucy.

"Aslan a man!" said Mr. Beaver sternly. "Certainly not. I tell you he is the King of the wood and the son of the great Emperor-Beyond-the-Sea. Don't you know who is the King of Beasts? Aslan is a lion—*the* lion, the great Lion."

"Ooh!" said Susan, "I'd thought he was a man. Is he—quite safe? I shall feel rather nervous about meeting a lion."

"That you will, dearie, and no mistake," said Mrs. Beaver; "if there's anyone who can appear before Aslan without their knees knocking, they're either braver than most or else just silly."

"Then he isn't safe?" said Lucy.

"Safe?" said Mr. Beaver; "don't you hear what Mrs. Beaver tells you? Who said anything about safe? 'Course he isn't safe. But he's good. He's the King, I tell you."

When we were young, most of us loved adventure. There is something about the unknown that draws us, which is why we like stories so much. But I like to leave the theater at the end of the play, knowing that the dilemma of evil has been resolved by the characters on the stage or screen. Like Peter, Susan, Lucy, and Edmund, to find ourselves not as spectators but as central characters in the play itself is somewhat daunting. The stakes are truly high, sometimes literally life or death, and God rarely if ever yells "Cut!" just as the dangerous or painful scene descends upon us. No stunt doubles come onto the set to take our places. Many of us feel that we have been playing these kinds of scenes ever since we were children. We wonder if the hero will ever show up to rescue us.

We would like to picture goodness as being synonymous with safety. When we think of God being good, we perhaps picture someone like Al on the popular TV program, *Home Improvement*. He is someone who carefully plans out each task ahead of time and has all the proper tools and safety equipment in place; someone who has thought out every possible danger ahead of time and made allowances to ensure our safety as his workmate; someone who goes to bed early, gets plenty of rest, and wears flannel shirts as a mark of his reliability.

Being in partnership with God, though, often feels much more like being Mel Gibson's sidekick in the movie *Lethal Weapon*. In his determination to deal with the bad guy, he leaps from seventh-story balconies into swimming pools, surprised that we would have any hesitation in following after him. Like Indiana Jones's love interests in the movies, we find ourselves caught up in an adventure of heroic proportions with a God who both seduces us with his boldness and energy and repels us with his willingness to place us in mortal danger, suspended over pits of snakes.

One strain of the modernist school of art is famous for creating "masterpieces" by standing back twenty feet and hurling paint onto the canvas. In answer to those who would criticize such a careless approach, they argue that chance is the real artist at work in this life and they do not want to interfere with its creative process. Our experience of what God is doing is sometimes felt from the perspective of one of those paint molecules. We come crashing onto the canvas who knows where, intermingled with whatever the fates bring along next.

Indeed, one of Satan's most powerful whisperings to us is that we are expendable. He may admit that we are part of God's plan for his own glory but only in the same way Napoleon used his soldiers to establish his empire. When the going got rough in the Russian winter campaign, Napoleon hightailed it back to Paris in his carriage, leaving Marshall Ney and the remnants of the once Grand Army to make it back the best way they could.

At one point in the long, arduous campaign of delivering to Judah the bad news of coming judgment and futile calls for repentance, Jeremiah explodes with thoughts that have apparently been building in him for a while with regard to God's use of him:

> O LORD, you deceived me, and I was deceived;
> you overpowered me and prevailed.
> I am ridiculed all day long;
> everyone mocks me.
> Whenever I speak, I cry out
> proclaiming violence and destruction.
> So the word of the LORD has brought me
> insult and reproach all day long.
> But if I say, "I will not mention him
> or speak any more in his name,"
> his word is in my heart like a fire,
> a fire shut up in my bones.
> I am weary of holding it in;
> indeed, I cannot. *(Jer. 20:7–9 NIV)*

Jeremiah complains that not only has God written a play that casts him in a devastating role, but that he has also placed a fire in his heart that will not let him leave the play even if he wants to. And there is this fire in all of us, felt as a desire for intimacy and a hunger for meaning, that we must literally kill if we want to escape the play.

To all of these charges, God is unrepentant, even as he was with Job. His response to these things is basically along the lines of, "I AM WHO I AM, I do what I do. I am good. What are you going to do with me?" Ironically, at the end of his interrogation by God, Job picks himself up and repents. He goes away with a sense of "Oh, now I get it. I was foolish to have lost perspective." God turns to Job's friends, who have been expounding the standard household-god formula to Job, "If you don't sin, things will go well [i.e., you can control your destiny]"—and tells them quite plainly they know nothing about him. He tells them he will have his *friend* Job pray for them.

Faced with the Message of the Arrows and a part too big that God the Cosmic Playwright insists is ours, with little clarity on the meaning and relationship of our scenes and character to the larger play, it appears more than sensible to opt out and go off-Broadway. Even though the smaller plays we write are often just pieces of stories, becoming our own directors and playwrights at least promises a level of control over the script. We hope we can eliminate most of the relational unknowns along with the villain and live in our smaller stories with some modicum of peace and quiet.

What is this drama God has dropped us into the middle of? What act of the play are we in and what do our scenes have to do with the larger story being told? Is our well-being even a consideration in the story line?

There is a stirring scene in Shakespeare's play *Henry V* that perhaps gives us a glimpse of what God is up to, both in the larger story he is telling as well as his purpose in our own lives, as he makes us a part of all this. Henry, the Christian king of England, has invaded France. After several battles, his army is worn down to six or seven thousand weary, hungry, and sick soldiers, dogged by rain and cold and thoughts of perhaps never seeing home again. The French army, fresh and thirty thousand strong, sends a courier to offer Henry the opportunity to avoid certain and ignominious defeat by surrendering. The hearts of Henry's army are divided as to the wisdom of battle. The king knows that hearts divided are hearts already defeated and he delivers a stirring speech on St. Crispin's day, capturing his soldiers' hearts up into something much larger:

> We would not die in that man's company
> That fears his fellowship to die with us.
> This day is call'd the feast of Crispian:
> He that outlives this day, and comes safe home,
> Will stand a tip-toe when this day is nam'd,
> And rouse him at the name of Crispian.
> He that shall live this day, and see old age,
> Will yearly on the vigil feast his neighbors,
> And say, tomorrow is Saint Crispian.
> Then will he strip his sleeve and show his scars,
> And say, These wounds I had on Crispin's day.
> Old men forget; yet all shall be forgot,
> But he'll remember with advantages
> What feats he did that day: then shall our names,
> Familiar in their mouths as household words . . .
> Be in their flowing cups freshly remember'd.
> This story shall the good man teach his son;
> And Crispin Crispian shall ne'er go by,
> From this day to the ending of the world,
> But we in it shall be remembered. (*Act IV, Scene III*)

Stirred to the core by the power of these words, Henry's men throw themselves into the battle with abandon and defeat the French in a total rout. King Henry calls his men to something that transcends safety and common sense. He calls them to battle and suffering that will bring them all a glorious remembering in the hearts of men. His words rouse something that burns within their hearts; something set there for the purposes of a king.

The battles God calls us to, the woundings and cripplings of soul and body we all receive, cannot simply be ascribed to our sin and foolishness, or even to the sin and foolishness of others. When Jesus and the disciples were on the road one day, they came upon a man who had been blind since birth. "Rabbi, who sinned, this man or his parents?" they asked him. "Neither this man nor his parents sinned," said Jesus, "but this happened so that the work of God might be displayed in his life." And with that, Jesus spat on the ground, made some mud to place on the man's eyes, and healed him (John 9:1–7).

Many of us who are reading these words have not yet received God's healing. The display of God's works through our wounds, losses, and sufferings is yet to be revealed. And so, we groan and we wonder.

A Strange Redemption

Yet there is something else God knows about us that causes him, like Henry V, to exhort us on into battle, or sometimes, even enter into battle against us. Most of us are convinced at some level in our heart that our main difficulty is the capriciousness of life. If we could ever overcome the damage of others' sins against us and just be loved better by those around us, and perhaps love a little better ourselves, we reason, we would be free to live well. For the most part, we don't see ourselves as people who are deeply committed to following the path to death. The way we want to live feels so right—so much like life—the only problem seems to be the way others treat us and God's indifference to our pleas for help. Some core part of all of our hearts is convinced that life would flow along smoothly if God were only a little more like those Mesopotamian household gods. The truth is, we all come into this world with a predilection to live life under our own terms and according to our own understanding.

We tell ourselves that we were not this way until the Arrows came and the Arrows certainly do deepen and justify our proclivity to reject God. Yet Jesus tells us through Paul in the third chapter of Romans that "There is no one righteous, not even one; there is no one who understands, no one who seeks God. All have turned away. . . ." (vv. 10–12). "There is a way that seems right to a man," says Proverbs 14:12, "but in the end it leads to death."

Genesis gives us an in-depth account of God using both crippling and blessing over the years of the patriarch Jacob's life to show him that his salvation and hope were in a more redemptive story than his own cleverness and manipulation could create; one that God was authoring. This is not the way we often see it, though. In our experience, it feels more as if God just allows bad things to happen to us out of indifference or malice. There is a fascinating illustration of a modern-day Jacob, a man trying to find redemption in a smaller story, along with God's fierce determination to disrupt and entice him back into the larger play, in the popular movie *Forrest Gump*. Forrest is a likable man of borderline intelligence who grew up struggling with leg braces due to polio and all of the cruel tauntings that those who are different often suffer. He is thrown into seemingly random scenes in American history much like the white feather that drifts with the wind throughout the movie. He finds himself in Vietnam under the leadership of Lieutenant Dan, a rough but capable man, whose family has produced a long line of military heroes killed in combat. Lieutenant Dan is confident that dying with honor on the field of battle is his redemption. When he is rescued by Forrest from a firefight, his wounds require both legs to be amputated above the knee. He and Forrest, also wounded, are consigned to the same hospital ward where one night the rageful Lieutenant Dan drags Forrest from his bed. He proceeds to choke and curse him for destroying his life by saving him.

"I was supposed to die on the battlefield, Gump!" rages Lieutenant Dan. "I used to be Lieutenant Dan. Now look at me. I'm just a . . . cripple."

In response, Forrest observes with poignant simplicity, "You *still* Lieutenant Dan," leaving him to collapse in grief and despair.

Lieutenant Dan, like all of us to one extent or another, is convinced that who he is, is inextricably tied to a self-redemptive story that alone will bring him recognition, honor, self-respect—indeed, salvation. When that is taken from him, he is engulfed by shame, anger, and despair. He goes to New York City and enters into a purgatorial story of his own making, killing all desire for redemption. He lives off of his veteran's benefits in a haze of alcohol, drugs, and sex with prostitutes. When Forrest comes to see him, Lieutenant Dan relates to him that some of the other veterans at the V.A. Hospital have been telling him he should trust in Jesus. "Can you believe it, Gump?" he remarks bitterly. "They tell me that Jesus will *walk* with me on the streets of heaven." But Lieutenant Dan can see no larger story than the one that has been stolen from him. He continues to pursue the destruction of his soul with the same zeal with which he once pursued glory on the battlefield.

On New Year's Eve, God the Wild One disrupts him again. Lieutenant Dan has corralled Forrest into going back to his apartment with two prostitutes to ring in the New Year with hedonistic disdain. The prostitutes play the game, each of them pretending great attraction to Lieutenant Dan and Forrest. When Forrest is uncomfortable with his "date's" advances, he clumsily resists. With the play she is acting out ruined, she spits out, "What's wrong with this retard?" and begins to berate Forrest.

And here, Lieutenant Dan finds out he has not been able to

totally kill his heart. He is filled with rage at this treatment of Forrest and orders both of the women to leave, prompting a barrage of derogatory epithets from them as they exit. With his heart again exposed, he is brought to the realization that he still cares. And with this realization, he is plunged into something beyond despair. The scene ends with a close-up of the death mask of his face stretched over a heart "filled" with inconsolable emptiness.

But God is not through with Lieutenant Dan.

Forrest travels to the Gulf of Mexico to try his hand at captaining a shrimp boat, a plan inherited from his army buddy, Benjamin Blue, who was killed in the same firefight that took Lieutenant Dan's legs. Forrest is bringing his boat back to the dock one afternoon after another fruitless day casting for shrimp. On the dock, cigar clenched in his teeth, his wheelchair adorned with an "America—My Kind of Place" sticker is Lieutenant Dan, ready to try his hand as Forrest's first mate.

The strangeness of hope has once again provoked him to another try at self-redemption from his self-imposed hell. But once again, the Divine Disrupter thwarts his efforts. Lieutenant Dan confidently directs Forrest to where he is sure the shrimp are hiding, only to have their nets repeatedly regurgitate onto the deck a collage of old tires, license plates, leather shoes, and a clam or two. By this time, Lieutenant Dan is convinced that God is working against him somehow. He passively assents to Forrest's petitioning the Almighty for his favor as a member of the congregation of an otherwise all-black church. As Forrest sways disharmoniously with the other choir members and handles the praying, Lieutenant Dan sits in the rear of the church, violently downing whiskey and waiting for Forrest to appease this uncooperative household god that has attached himself to his life.

The ensuing days' shrimping brings no more harvest than before. With storm clouds gathering in the background, a completely frustrated and furious Lieutenant Dan rages, "Where . . . is this God of yours, Gump? I wish your Jesus were here right now!" And Forrest comments to his listeners with rare irony, "It's funny Lieutenant Dan said that 'cause right then, God showed up." God sends a storm that puts the boat in mortal danger of being destroyed. Unbowed, Lieutenant Dan lashes himself to the mast, filled with joy at this opportunity to finally have it out with his tormenter. He curses God and dares him to sink the boat. But God has another purpose for Lieutenant Dan. He allows the storm to rage until his anger is spent but does not kill him. Later, we learn that Forrest and Lieutenant Dan's boat has been the only survivor in the entire shrimping fleet. As they once again ply the shrimping grounds, now without competition, their hoists and nets strain to release one cascading swarm of shrimp after another onto the deck of their boat.

As Forrest recounts the story of their becoming millionaires to a credulous but kind lady at a bus stop, he asks if she would like to know what happened to Lieutenant Dan. As he describes the scene to her, we see Lieutenant Dan sitting on the rail of their shrimping boat. The anger and fear so long entrenched there are gone. In their place is a kind of reflective surprise, like that of a man who has been redeemed in a most unexpected way. "Forrest," says Lieutenant Dan in a quiet, almost shy voice, "I never thanked you for saving my life." And with that, he hoists his legless body over the side. As Forrest hurries to the rail with some concern over his intentions, we see Lieutenant Dan backstroking peacefully through the water with a gentle smile on his face. As the camera moves away, we leave him swimming up the reflected gold highway of the sunset on the water, even as Forrest remarks, "I think Lieutenant Dan finally made his peace with God."

And again, we wonder. What is it that Lieutenant Dan has discovered? What healing has he received even though his legs are unrestored?

So often, like Lieutenant Dan before his healing, we feel
that God is not only unconcerned with our plight, but that he
is actually working against us. And sometimes, we are right. The
story of Lieutenant Dan is a poignant and revealing portrayal of
God's fierce intentions to use both crippling and blessing to
redeem us from our self-redemptive and purgatorial stories.
Indeed, in the seventeenth chapter of Acts, Paul gives the Athe-
nians the stunning news that every single thing in the lives of
both nations and individuals is orchestrated with this sole objective that they might seek God (vv. 26–28). This revelation
requires some reflection. We are used to thinking of the great
movements of history, even the movements in our immediate
relationships, as being impersonal, if not arbitrary. But with
God, who notes the fall of every sparrow, the events of our lives
are thoughtfully and thoroughly orchestrated to bring about
our redemption. The days of our lives were ordered and num-
bered before there was one of them, says the psalmist (139:16).
And yet, the ways of his redemption often leave us trembling
and fearful.

Frederick Buechner, in his novel *Son of Laughter*, nonetheless invites us to relationship with this Wild Deity through the
words of Jacob. Jacob's journey has come full circle, the smaller
story he was attempting to live through deception and manipulation has been rewritten by the purposes of the Wild Romancer
who is God. He is once again in need of redemption, his sons,
Simeon and Levi, having just murdered Hamor and Shechem
along with all their people for the rape of their sister, Dinah.
Jacob is ready to let Simeon and Levi die in turn to cleanse
(redeem) his family from the curse of the household gods
Rachel (his wife) stole from her father's house, having brought
them with her on this journey home.

Instead, the Fear (the only name by which Jacob knows
God) commands him to sacrifice a red heifer and use the ashes
to purify his sons and himself. Noting that they are cleansed on

the outside, Jacob laments that the household gods still control them internally with their promises of earthbound blessing. He exhorts his family to give the Fear their hearts' trust even as he buries all the household gods under the oak tree where Abraham so long ago built his altar in memory of the three angels come to pledge him God's covenant. Here are Jacob's words to us through Buechner:

> The unclean blood no longer clung to our hands, but the small gods clung still to our hearts. They clung with silver fingers, with fingerless hands of wood and baked clay. Like rats, the gods gibbered in our hearts about the rich gifts they have for giving to us. The gods give rain. The swelling udder they give and the sweet fig, the plump ear of grain, the ooze of oil. They give sons. To Laban they gave cunning. They give their names as the Fear, at the Jabbok, refused me his when I asked it, and a god named is a god summoned. The Fear comes when he comes. It is the Fear who summons. The gods give in return for your gifts to them: the strangled dove, the burnt ox, the first fruit. There are those who give them their firstborn even, the child bound to the altar for knifing as Abraham bound Isaac till the Fear of his mercy bade the urine-soaked old man unbind him. The Fear gives to the empty-handed, the empty-hearted, as to me from the stone stair he gave promise and blessing, and gave them also to Isaac before me, to Abraham before Isaac, all of us wanderers only, herdsmen and planters moving with the seasons as gales of dry sand move with the wind. In return it is only the heart's trust that the Fear asks. Trust him though you cannot see him and he has no silver hand to hold. Trust him though you have no name to call him by, though out of the black night he leaps like a stranger to cripple and bless.

"Do you really care for me, God?"

Can we trust this stranger who leaps out upon us? Could it be that his glory and our well-being really are part of the same script?

If only we understood his heart more clearly. . . .

6

God the Ageless Romancer

So long as we imagine it is we who have to look for God, we must often lose heart. But it is the other way about—He is looking for us.

Simon Tugwell

CAN IT POSSIBLY get any more uncertain than this? We so long for life to be better than it is. We wish the beauty and love and adventure would stay and that someone strong and kind would show us how to make the Arrows go away. We hope that God will be our hero. Of all the people in the universe, he could stop the Arrows and arrange for just a little more blessing in our lives. He can spin the earth, change the weather, topple governments, obliterate armies, and resurrect the dead. Is it too much to ask that he intervene in our story? But he often seems aloof, almost indifferent to our plight, so entirely out of our control. Would it be any worse if there were no God? If he didn't exist, at least we wouldn't get our hopes up. We could settle once and for all that we really are alone in the universe and get on with surviving as best we may.

This is, in fact, how many professing Christians end up living: as practical agnostics. *Perhaps God will come through, perhaps he won't, so I'll be hanged if I'll live as though he had to come through. I'll hedge my bets and if he does show up, so much the better.* The simple word for this is *godlessness.* Like a lover who's been wronged, we guard our heart against future disappointment.

In my sophomore year in high school I (John) fell in love with a beautiful junior named Joy. Our first dates were romantic, exciting, and full of adventure. I gave her my heart. One day several months into the relationship, I was trying in vain to thumb a ride home when I saw her car approaching. My heart leaped with anticipation, but Joy whizzed past in her convertible with another guy at the wheel. Adding insult to injury, she waved gaily as they rushed by. I felt the fool, which is what we often do when we feel betrayed. And I never gave her my heart again.

Everyone has been betrayed by someone, some more profoundly than others. Betrayal is a violation that strikes at the core of our being; to make ourselves vulnerable and entrust our well-being to another, only to be harmed by those on whom our hopes were set, is among the worst pain of human experience.

Sometimes the way God treats us feels like betrayal. We find ourselves in a dangerous world, unable to arrange for the water our thirsty souls so desperately need. Our rope won't take the bucket to the bottom of the well. We know God has the ability to draw water for us, but oftentimes he won't. We feel wronged. After all, doesn't Scripture say that if we have the power to do someone good, we should do it (Prov. 3:27)? So why doesn't God?

As I spoke with a friend about her painful life, how reckless and unpredictable God seems, she turned and with pleading eyes asked the question we are all asking somewhere deep within: "How can I trust a lover who is so wild?" Indeed, how do we not only trust him, but love him in return? There's only one possible answer: You could love him if you *knew* his heart was good. In the movie *The Last of the Mohicans*, brave Nathaniel has captured the heart of the beautiful Cora. With tremendous courage and cunning, he rescues her from an ambush set by the black-hearted Magua, leader of a warring tribe. Nathaniel leads Cora, her sister, and a few other survivors to a hidden cave behind a waterfall. Just when it appears they will escape and live happily ever after, Magua and his savages discover their hideout. Once captured, the women may be spared but the men will surely be executed. With no powder for their rifles, Nathaniel's only chance is to leap from the falls; by saving himself, he will live to rescue Cora another day. One of the other men calls him a coward, accusing him of foul and selfish motives. How is Cora feeling? What looks like abandonment may not be. Her only hope in the face of such wildness lies in the goodness of Nathaniel's heart. At this point, it's all she has to go on. It's all we often have to go on too.

Does God have a good heart? In the last chapter Brent spoke of God as the Author of the story, which is how most people see him if they see him at all. And, as Hamlet said, there's the rub. When we think of God as Author, the Grand Chess Player, the Mind Behind It All, we doubt his heart. As Melville said, "The reason the mass of men fear God and at bottom dislike him is because they rather distrust his heart, and fancy him all brain, like a watch." Do you relate to the author when reading a novel or watching a film? Caught up in the action, do you even think about the author? We identify with the characters in the story precisely because they are *in* the story. They face life as we do, on the ground, and their struggles win our sympathy because they are our struggles also. We love the hero because he is one of us, and yet somehow rises above the fray to be better and wiser and more loving as we hope one day we might prove to be.

The Author lies behind, beyond. His omniscience and omnipotence may be what create the drama, but they are also what separate us from him. Power and knowledge don't qualify for heart. Indeed, the worst sort of villain is the kind who executes his plans with cold and calculated precision. He is detached; he has no heart. If we picture God as the mastermind behind the story—calling the shots while we, like Job, endure the calamities—we can't help but feel at times what C. S. Lewis was bold enough to put words to: "We're the rats in the cosmic laboratory." Sure, he may have our good in mind, but that still makes him the "vivisectionist"—the experimenter.

We root for the hero and heroine, even come to love them, because they are living *in* the drama. They feel the heartache, they suffer loss and summon courage and shed their own blood in their struggles against evil. What if? Just what if we saw God not as Author, the cosmic mastermind behind all human experience, but as the central character *in* the larger story? What could we learn about his heart?

I worked as an actor in Los Angeles for a number of years. In the theater, when you're preparing to act a part, you want to "get into the skin" of your character, to discover his motives. What makes him tick? Why does he do the things he does? Every human action has a motive behind it. Nathaniel jumps from the waterfall, leaving Cora behind. Why? He lives to fight another day. Why does he live to fight again? Beneath simple motives lie deeper purposes. What is it that drives this hero throughout the course of his life? His love for Cora. Here might be the key to our dilemma: The Scriptures are written from the perspective that God is the hero of the story. Let's revisit the drama with the view of God as lead actor. What is his motive? How does life affect him?

The Larger Story

Act I: His Eternal Heart

All good fairy tales begin with "Once upon a time," and so it is with the truest fairy tale of all. *In the beginning*, which is to say, once upon a time, is used twice in the Scriptures. There is the first verse of Genesis, of course, but we cannot start there because when the curtain goes up on Genesis chapter 1, it is actually going up on later events, the human story. We're after God's story, the drama from his perspective, so we would do better to start with the opening lines from the gospel of John, which take us back even farther to the once upon a time before time: "In the beginning was the Word, and the Word was with God, and the Word was God. He was with God in the beginning."

The story that is the Sacred Romance begins not with God alone, the Author at his desk, but God in relationship, intimacy beyond our wildest imagination, heroic intimacy. The Trinity is at the center of the universe; perfect relationship is the heart of all reality. Think of your best moments of love or friendship or creative partnership, the best times with family or friends around the dinner table, your richest conversations, the acts of simple kindness that sometimes seem like the only things that make life worth living. Like the shimmer of sunlight on a lake, these are reflections of the love that flows among the Trinity. We long for intimacy because we are made in the image of perfect intimacy. Still, what we don't have and may never have known is often a more powerful reminder of what *ought* to be.

Our story begins with the hero in love. As Buechner reminds us, "God does not need the Creation in order to have something to love because within himself love happens."

And yet, what kind of love? There are selfish forms of love, relationships that create closed systems, impenetrable to outsiders. Real love creates a generous openness. Have you ever been so caught up in something that you just had to share it? When you are walking alone in the woods, something takes your breath away—a sunset, a waterfall, the simple song of a bird—and you think, *If only my beloved were here*. The best things in life were meant to be shared. That is why married lovers want to increase their joy by having children. And so it is with God.

"Father," Jesus says, "I want those you gave me to be with me, right where I am. I want them to be one heart and mind with us" (John 17). Overflowing with the generosity that comes from the abundance of real love, he creates us to share in the joy of this heroic intimacy. One early mystic says we were created out of the laughter of the Trinity.

Sunday afternoons were my favorite days during summers on my grandfather's ranch. That's when we'd go "visiting," calling on second cousins, great aunts, adopted friends, and other relatives at their farms. I remember having a warm, settled feeling as I sat on the porch and listened to the older folks remembering the shared stories of their lives. My sense of security grew from an awareness that all this had been going on before me, that though I was part of it, I wasn't responsible for it. It didn't depend on me. You've heard that children care more that their parents love each other than that they love them and this is the reason why. It's the assurance that there is something grand and good going on that doesn't rest on your shoulders, something that doesn't even culminate in you, but rather invites you up into it.

And so it is with God's story. Before any of our complex and sometimes overwhelming smaller stories began, there was something wonderful already going on: Once upon a time, were Father, Son, and Holy Spirit—the kind of home we've been looking for all our life. From the beginning, we know that God is a lover at heart, from all eternity.

Act II: His Heart Betrayed

There was another scene before ours. In Act II, there came angels. We're not given a great deal of insight into the life of angels, but we do know that God opened his heart and home to a heavenly host before us. And for the most part, they seem thrilled to be a part of things. Scripture never shows us a bored angel. Quite the contrary. We also know there was a cosmic divorce, a betrayal in the heart of the universe. Satan, then named Lucifer, turned on his Maker. He rose up against his sovereign Lord, and with him legions upon legions of angels. There was war in heaven. In *Paradise Lost*, John Milton wrestled with the heights of poetic imagery to capture the drama of this scene:

> How shall I relate
> To human sense th' invisible exploits
> Of warring spirits? how, without remorse,
> The ruin of so many, glorious once
> And perfect while they stood.

He tells the story of a majestic heavenly banquet thrown by the Father in honor of the Son. The first member of the Trinity, generous of heart, freely gives center stage to the second member of the Trinity. Satan is unable to endure the glory bestowed on Jesus. Satan is jealous for himself and this kind always ends in murder. Believing that he should have center stage, Satan draws a multitude of angels into battle against the throne of God:

> Arms on armor clashing brayed
> Horrible discord; dire was the noise
> Of conflict; overhead the dismal hiss
> Of fiery darts in flaming volleys flew
> So under fiery cope together rushed
> Both battles main with ruinous assault
> And inextinguishable rage. All heaven
> Resounded; and, had earth been then, all earth
> Had to her centre shook.
> Deeds of eternal fame were done,
> But infinite; for wide was spread
> That war, and various; sometimes on firm ground
> A standing fight; then, soaring on main wing
> Tormented all the air; and all air seemed then
> Conflicting fire. Long time in even scale
> The battle hung, till Satan
> No equal, ranging through the dire attack

Of fighting seraphim confused, at length
Saw where the sword of Michael smote, and felled
Squadrons at once; with huge two-handed sway.

At the approach of Satan, the great archangel Michael "from his warlike toil surceased," turning to confront the betrayer of their heaven:

Author of evil, unknown till thy revolt . . .
How hast thou disturbed
Heaven's blessed peace, and unto Nature brought
Misery, uncreated till the crime
Of thy rebellion. How hast thou instilled
Thy malice into thousands, once upright
And faithful, now proved false . . .
Heaven casts thee out.

Satan mounted his rebellion through the power of one idea: God doesn't have a good heart. Though it seems almost incomprehensible, he deceived a multitude of the heavenly host by sowing the seed of doubt in their minds that God was somehow holding out on them. After the insurrection is squelched, that question lingers in the universe like smoke from a forest fire. Sure, God won, but it took force to do it. Power isn't the same thing as goodness. As the lead actor in the story, God *seems* generous and self-giving, but perhaps he's just big. Maybe his motive is simply to be in charge. At the end of Act II, our hero's heart has been called into question.

Act III: His Heart on Trial

When the curtain goes up on the story of humanity, we see God in a flurry of breathtaking dramatic actions that we rather blandly call "creation." Remember, we're looking for the motives of his heart. Why is he doing all this? We know he already had the perfect relationship and that he has suffered a betrayal in the heart of heaven simply for the offense of sharing it. Now we see him preparing to woo our hearts with a world that is beautiful and funny and full of adventure. Don't rush ahead to the Fall. Stay here a moment and feel God's happiness with it all. Yosemite and Yellowstone and Maui and the Alps; mangoes and blackberries and cabernet grapes; horses and hummingbirds and rainbow trout. "The morning stars sang together and all the angels shouted for joy" (Job 38:7 NIV).

God creates man and woman and sets them in Paradise. How long had he been planning this? Are we merely the replacement for the angels he lost, the first date he can find on the rebound? The first chapter of Ephesians gives a look into God's motives here:

> Long before he laid down earth's foundations, he had us in mind, had settled on us as the focus of his love, to be made whole and holy by his love. Long, long ago he decided to adopt us into his family through Jesus Christ. (What pleasure he took in planning this!) He wanted us to enter into the celebration of his lavish gift-giving by the hand of his beloved Son. . . . Long before we first heard of Christ and got our hopes up, he had his eye on us, had designs on us for glorious living. (*The Message*)

God begins our courtship with a surprise. Taking the blindfold off, he turns us around and reveals his handmade wedding present. "Here," he says. "It's yours. Enjoy yourselves. Do you like it? Take it for a spin." A lavish gift indeed. What's he up to? Flowers, chocolates, exotic vacations, dinners at the finest restaurants—any person would feel pursued. But what are his intentions? Surprisingly, we see in the first glimpse of God's wildness the goodness of his heart—he gives us our freedom. In order for a true romance to occur, we had to be free to reject him. In *Disappointment with God*, Philip Yancey reminds us that the powers of the Author aren't sufficient to win our hearts.

> Power can do everything but the most important thing: it cannot control love. . . . In a concentration camp, the guards possess almost unlimited power. By applying force, they can make you renounce your God, curse your family, work without pay, eat

human excrement, kill and then bury your closest friend or even your own mother. All this is within their power. Only one thing is not: they cannot force you to love them. This fact may help explain why God sometimes seems shy to use his power. He created us to love him, but his most impressive displays of miracle—the kind we may secretly long for—do nothing to foster that love. As Douglas John Hall has put it, "God's problem is not that God is not able to do certain things. God's problem is that God loves. Love complicates the life of God as it complicates every life."

The wildness of giving us freedom is even more staggering when we remember that God has already paid dearly for giving freedom to the angels. But because of his grand heart he goes ahead and takes the risk, an enormous, colossal risk. The reason he didn't make puppets is because he wanted lovers. Remember, he's inviting us up into a romance. Freedom is part of the explanation for the problem of evil. God is the author of some storms directly; but he is the author of the possibility of all storms in giving us freedom. And *we* opened Pandora's box.

Can you imagine if on your honeymoon one of you sneaked off for a rendezvous with a perfect stranger? Adam and Eve kicked off the honeymoon by sleeping with the enemy. Then comes one of the most poignant verses in all Scripture. "What is this you have done?" (Gen. 3:13). You can almost hear the shock, the pain of betrayal in God's voice. The fall of Adam and Eve mustn't be pictured as a crime like theft, but as a betrayal of love. In love God creates us for love and we give him the back of our hand. Why? Satan gets us to side with him by sowing the seed of doubt in our first parents' minds: "God's heart really isn't good. He's holding out on you. You've got to take things into your own hands." And Paradise was lost.

Yet there was something about the heart of God that the angels and our first parents had not yet seen. Here, at the lowest point in our relationship, God announces his intention never to abandon us but to seek us out and win us back. "I will come for you." *Grace* introduces a new element of God's heart. Up till this point we knew he was rich, famous, influential, even generous. Behind all that can still can hide a heart that is less than good. Grace removes all doubt.

And then the long story of God's pursuit of humanity begins. Satan wanted center stage: He wanted to be the main character, he wanted to be the point. His plan now is to ruin the Sacred Romance, to get us all caught up in our own little socio-dramas by telling us that we are the point. You can see how humanity goes along with this. Cain murders Abel; Lamech threatens to murder everyone else. Humanity grows worse and worse until God says in pain, "I'm sorry I ever made them." But he doesn't give up. First with Noah, then Abraham, then Israel, we see God pursuing a people whose hearts will be for him, with whom he can share the joy of the larger story. But their faithfulness lasts about as long as the morning dew.

How is God feeling by this point? As a person *in the story*, what is his heart experience? When we reach the prophets, we get a glimpse at what it feels like to be God. Reading the prophets, says Yancey, is like hearing a lovers' quarrel through the apartment wall. Eavesdrop on the argument and catch a glimpse of his heart:

> I long to be gracious to you. You are precious and honored in my sight, because I love you. But you—come here, you . . . you . . . offspring of adulterers. You have made your bed on a high and lofty hill, forsaking me, you uncovered your bed, you climbed into it and opened it wide. You have been false to me. Yet . . . I will take delight in you, as a bridegroom rejoices over his bride, so will I rejoice over you. *(From Isaiah)*

> I remember the devotion of your youth, how as a bride you loved me. . . . What fault did you find in me that you strayed so far from me? You are a swift she-camel running here and there, sniffing the wind in her craving—in her heat who can restrain her? Should I not punish them for this? Should I not avenge myself? I have loved you with an everlasting love; I have drawn you with lovingkindness. What have I done to make you hate me so much? *(From Jeremiah)*

I will answer you according to your idols [your false lovers] in order to recapture your heart. *(From Ezekiel)*

Return to me and I will return to you. Yet you have said harsh things about me. You have said, "There's no pay-off in this relationship. It's not worth loving God." *(From Malachi)*

After this, four hundred years of silence. God doesn't call and when we do he won't answer the phone. You can almost imagine him nursing his wounds, wondering where it all went wrong. And then an idea comes to him. Here is Kierkegaard's version of the story:

Suppose there was a king who loved a humble maiden. The king was like no other king. Every statesman trembled before his power. No one dared breathe a word against him, for he had the strength to crush all opponents. And yet this mighty king was melted by love for a humble maiden. How could he declare his love for her? In an odd sort of way, his kingliness tied his hands. If he brought her to the palace and crowned her head with jewels and clothed her body in royal robes, she would surely not resist—no one dared resist him. But would she love him?

She would say she loved him, of course, but would she truly? Or would she live with him in fear, nursing a private grief for the life she had left behind? Would she be happy at his side? How could he know? If he rode to her forest cottage in his royal carriage, with an armed escort waving bright banners, that too would overwhelm her. He did not want a cringing subject. He wanted a lover, an equal. He wanted her to forget that he was a king and she a humble maiden and to let shared love cross the gulf between them. For it is only in love that the unequal can be made equal. (as quoted in *Disappointment with God*)

The king clothes himself as a beggar and renounces his throne in order to win her hand. The Incarnation, the life and the death of Jesus, answers once and for all the question, "What is God's heart toward me?" This is why Paul says in Romans 5, "Look here, at the Cross. Here is the demonstration of God's heart. At the point of our deepest betrayal, when we had run our farthest from him and gotten so lost in the woods we could never find our way home, God came and died to rescue us." We don't have to wait for the Incarnation to see God as a character in the story and learn something of his motives. But after the Incarnation there can be no doubt.

There is so much more to say. Jesus left to prepare our place in heaven; the Spirit has come to empower us to continue the invasion of the kingdom, which is primarily about freeing the hearts of others to live in the love of God. There is so much in our own heart that remains to be released. Our enemy has not given up yet and his target is also our heart. And what of Act IV, the coming adventures of heaven? All that is for the chapters ahead. Let's stop here and try to bring this into focus.

What is God like? Is his heart good? We know he is the initiator from first to last. As Simon Tugwell reminds, God is the one pursuing us:

> So long as we imagine that it is we who have to look for God, we must often lose heart. But it is the other way about; He is looking for us. And so we can afford to recognize that very often we are not looking for God; far from it, we are in full flight from him, in high rebellion against him. And He knows that and has taken it into account. He has followed us into our own darkness; there where we thought finally to escape him, we run straight into his arms. So we do not have to erect a false piety for ourselves, to give us the hope of salvation. Our hope is in his determination to save us, and he will not give in. (*Prayer*)

When we feel that life is finally up to us it becomes suffocating. When we are the main character, the world is so small there's barely room to move. It frees our souls to have something going on before us that involves us, had us in mind, yet doesn't depend on us or culminate in us, but invites us up into something larger. And what about the Romance and the Arrows? It wasn't supposed to be like this. Once upon a time we lived in a garden; we lived in the place for which we were made. There were no Arrows, only beauty. Our relationships weren't tainted with fear, guardedness, manipulation, quid pro quo. Our work was rewarding; we received more than we gave. There is beauty, and we so long for it to last; we were made for the Garden. But now there is affliction also, and that is because we live East of Eden. The Arrows seem like the truest part of life, but they are not. The heart of the universe is still perfect love.

Finally, if we try to relate to God primarily as Author, we will go mad or despair—pretty much the same thing. I just can't imagine the characters of a novel affecting the author that much. He may like them, hate them, be intrigued with mapping out their development, but they don't impact him the way the people in his real life do. He doesn't live with them as flesh-and-blood lovers. But when we see God as the Hero of the story and consider what he wants for us, we know one thing for certain: We affect him. We impact the members of the Trinity as truly as they do each other.

It is only when we see God as the Hero of the larger story that we come to know his heart is good.

Where does that leave us? What is our role in the cosmic drama? Are we bit players, added for dramatic tension, color, comic relief? Neil Anderson has written that while "The most important belief we possess is true knowledge of who God is. . . . The second most important belief is who we are as children of God." In the next chapter, we'll explore our role in the story.

7

The Beloved

I am my beloved's and his desire is for me.
Song of Songs

HELEN OF TROY must have really been something. Two kingdoms went to war over her; thousands of men gave up their lives so that one might have her. Hers was "the face that launched a thousand ships." Helen was the wife of Menelaus, King of Greece, in the ninth Century, B.C. Their home was a peaceful mediterranean kingdom until the arrival of Paris, Prince of Troy. Paris fell in love with Helen and, depending on the version of the story you've heard, she with him. Under the cover of night, Paris stole away with Helen and took her back to Troy. It was the beginning of the Trojan War. Menelaus and his brother Agamemnon amassed a mighty Greek army and set off in one thousand ships to lay siege on Troy, all to win Helen back.

Few have ever felt so pursued. Sometimes we wonder if we've even been *noticed*. Father was too busy to come to our games, or perhaps he jumped ship altogether. Mother was lost in a never-ending pile of laundry or, more recently, in her own career. We come into the world longing to be special to someone and from the start we are disappointed. It is a rare soul indeed who has been sought after for who she is—not because of what she can do, or what others can gain from her, but simply for herself. Can you recall a time when a significant someone in your life sat you down with the sole purpose of wanting to know your heart more deeply, fully expecting to enjoy what he found there? More people have climbed Mt. Everest than have experienced real pursuit, and so what are we left to conclude? There is nothing in our hearts worth knowing. Whoever and whatever this mystery called *I* must be, it cannot be much.

"In fact," we continue, "if I am not pursued, it must be because there is something wrong with me, something dark and twisted inside.' We long to be known and we fear it like nothing else. Most people live with a subtle dread that one day they will be discovered for who they really are and the world will be appalled.

The wife of a close friend was seeing a counselor to sort through some of her own Arrows. After several private sessions she asked her husband, who is a pastor, to come along. As the day of the event drew near, his quiet dread swelled to full-fledged panic. The night before their joint session the pastor had a dream in which the counselor uncovered his true self, then leaped up from her chair and ran out of the office and down the street, screaming, "My God—he's a pastor!"

We come into the world with a longing to be known and a deep-seated fear that we aren't what we should be. We are set up for a crisis of identity. And then, says Frederick Buechner, the world goes to work:

> Starting with the rather too pretty young woman and the charming but rather unstable young man, who together know no more about being parents than they do the far side of the moon, the world sets in to making us what the world would like us to be, and because we have to survive after all, we try to make ourselves into something that we hope the world will like better than it apparently did the selves we originally were. That is the story of all our lives, needless to say, and in the process of living out that story, the original, shimmering self gets buried so deep that most of us hardly

end up living out of it at all. Instead, we live out all the other selves which we are constantly putting on and taking off like coats and hats against the world's weather. (*Telling Secrets*)

Think about the part you find yourself playing, the self you put on like a costume. Who cast you in this role? Most of us are living out a script that someone else has written for us. We've not been invited to live from our heart, to be who we truly are, so we put on these false selves hoping to offer something more acceptable to the world, something functional. We learn our roles starting very young and we learn them well: Joey's the smart kid and his role is to be smart. He'll help you with your homework and grow up to be a computer programmer. Karen is the victim of abuse, struggling against overwhelming odds. She's been given the role of being used. The pretty girls get to be the cheerleaders, the others are sent to the library. The athletic boys are picked for the team, the others are simply picked on. Either we're chosen for the wrong reasons or not chosen at all.

What does any of this have to do with our heart? God created each of us with a unique identity, a role in the larger story, but early on we've been handed a revision by the other players in our life.

"Well, then," the realist might say, "don't let people affect you so much. Be your own person. Believe in yourself." Those who've tried realize that this advice just isn't enough for the healing of your soul and the recovery of your true identity. The deepest Arrows we've known are lodged in the places of our self-identity and no amount of positive thinking or self-affirmation will remove them. There are words that have been spoken, repeated a thousand times, and they play like a recording in our inner thoughts: "stupid," "incompetent," "ugly," "unlovable"—the list goes on and on.

There are images, too, scenes from our lives that speak more deeply even than words. In the second grade I (John) wet my pants in school one day. We were watching a film and I was too embarrassed to interrupt class to ask permission to leave. I tried to hold it as long as I could, but the film was longer. A puddle formed beneath my desk. Mortified, fearing the Arrows of playground taunts, I tried a cover-up and claimed my thermos had broken. The teacher sent me to the office for the nurse to call my parents to bring a pair of dry pants. No one was home. In a moment of real need, when I so desperately wanted someone to be there for me, I was alone. Something clicked within me; an image settled in that place, which captured the message that I had better never blow it again because there wouldn't be anyone to pick me up when I fell. So much of my perfectionism as an adult is energized by that image: Never be in a place of need.

Deep within the Arrows stay, poisoning our self-percep-tions, until someone comes along with the power to take them away, free us from all the false selves we use to weather the world's weather, and restore to us our true identity. Without such a person, we are lost in the smaller stories, anxiously look-ing about, hoping for a clue as to who we really are. We read the opinions that others hold of us like a report card on how we're doing. Parents of teenagers warn them against the rip-tides of peer pressure, but who of us does not to some degree succumb? Fashion is an enduring testimony to the fact that we live quite consciously before the eyes of others. And for such we were made. We were created to live in community, not a hall of mirrors. Philosopher and author Gabriel Marcel uses an experience from daily life to reveal the way in which we estab-lish a sense of self:

> Take, for instance, the child who brings his mother flowers he has just been gathering in the meadow. "Look," he cries, "I picked these." Mark the triumph in his voice and above all the gesture . . . which accompanies his announcement. The child points himself out for admiration and gratitude: "It was I, I who am with you

here, who picked these lovely flowers, don't go thinking it was Nanny or my sister; it was I and *no one else*." (*Homo Viator*)

Luke, my two-year-old, found me one Saturday morning puttering in the garage. "'Mere," he said, in a tone and with an expression that allowed no room for debate. He turned and I followed him into the family room. "Sit." I sat down, my curiosity fully engaged. "Watch!" He climbed onto his Won-derColt and began to ride with great passion, a cowboy on some dangerous mission in which he would be the hero. Something outside the window drew my attention and I looked away, a very big mistake. "Watch *me*!" he demanded. Luke wanted what we all want—to play our part, to live our lives before the eyes of another. Actually, he wanted more than simple recognition. He wanted praise, admiration, applause—in short, he wanted glory.

How could it be otherwise? We are created in the image of God, or more precisely, *as a reflection of the Trinity*. If we really understood this wonderful truth deep in our hearts, it would probably bring revival in our day. Consider just two essential realities that flow from this fact. First, as we observed in the previous chapter, the Trinity is a community and so to be made in its image means we are relational at our core. "Our creation is by love, in love and for love," writes psychologist Gerald May. But there is more. The Trinity is a society whose members draw their identities from the others. The Father wouldn't be a father if it weren't for his relationship to the Son and to us. He might be "God," "Jehovah," even "Almighty," but never "Abba, Father." Of course the Son would never have been one if not for the presence of the Father. But because of his relationship to the other members of the Trinity, Jesus has been and forever will be the Son of God. And just like my son, Luke, and all children, what he craves most, his greatest prize, is the applause of the Father. "Father, I want those you have given me to be with me where I am, and to see my glory, the glory you have given me because you loved me before the creation of the world" (John 17:24).

Identity is not something that falls on us out of the sky. For better or for worse, identity is *bestowed*. We are who we are in relation to others. But far more important, we draw our identity from our impact on those others—*if* and *how* we affect them. We long to know that we make a difference in the lives of others, to know that we matter, that our presence cannot be replaced by a pet, a possession, or even another person. The awful burden of the false self is that it must be constantly maintained. What happened to Helen of Troy when her hips began to bulge and her face sag? Did she leap from bed each morning to the mirror, fearing that the effects of the passing years would make her less and less lovable? Our dilemma is hers: We think we have to keep doing something in order to be desirable. Once we find something that will bring us some attention, we have to keep it going or risk the loss of the attention.

And so we live with the fear of not being chosen and the burden of maintaining whatever it is about us that might get us noticed and the commitment never to be seen for who we really are. We develop a *functional* self-image, even if it is a negative one. The little boy paints his red wagon a speckled gray with whatever Father left in the can after putting a new coat on the backyard fence. "Look what I did!" he says, hoping for affirmation of the wonderful impact his presence has on the world. The angry father shames him: "What do you think you're doing? You've ruined it." The boy forms an identity: *My impact is awful; I foul good things up. I am a fouler.* And he forms a commitment never to be in a place where he can foul things up again. Years later, his colleagues wonder why he turned down an attractive promotion. The answer lies in his identity, an identity he received from the impact he had on the most important person in his world and his fear of ever being in such a place again.

A little girl draws her father's attention only when he wants to use her for his sexual perversions. *I am sexually dangerous,* she concludes. *I am a dirty little girl.* She lives with the tremendous rift in her soul caused by the ambivalence of abuse. On the one hand, the attention felt good. She was made for intimacy. Yet the only intimacy she's ever known was violating. Years later, she becomes the efficient, competent head of women's ministry at church. She's known as a tireless worker and a real servant—but there isn't a man who is drawn to her in any intimate way. She carefully avoids all compliments and keeps any potential relationships at a purely "ministry" level. She can't take the risk of being attractive sexually. Long ago she learned that intimacy leads to violation, that the sensual parts of her are dirty and so she hides them well beneath a false self of Christian service.

For the past thirty years, I have found my identity and earned my living by being up front, first as an actor, then as a public speaker. That script began in the second grade when I fell in love with my teacher, Mrs. McGrath. She was young and pretty and she *noticed* me, noticed that I could speak well in front of the class and so she picked me to narrate the school play. Something deep within me was stirred, touched. I gave a brilliant reading and all the mothers cried. *Ahha!* my little foolish heart concluded, *this is my part—this is how I will find glory!* And for thirty years I have lived out that part, rarely offering the truest parts of me and so rarely feeling alive and connected with anyone. You cannot have intimacy out of a false self.

There is no escaping your identity. You will not live beyond how you see yourself; not for long. If "Failure" is the part you're playing, you will fail. The Performers will perform, the Seductive will seduce, the Victims will be victimized, the Nobodies will fade away, and the Somebodies will do whatever it is that made them feel like somebody, donning coat and hat according to the weather. Again, what we are doing in this costume ball of life is looking to avoid exposure while at the same time trying to offer something that will bring us glory.

As a young girl my friend Susan was lost in a busy household full of brothers and sisters and seldom seen by distracted parents. One day she made a necklace from pumpkin seeds, a simple craft to pass the time. For some odd reason the necklace captured her father's attention. "Hey, everybody, look at this, will ya? Look at what Susan made!" Years later, as she reflected back on what seemed a trivial moment, she remembered the power she seemed to suddenly possess: "People came alive at something I did!" Does it come as a surprise to learn that she is now makes her living as a creative designer?

It's not that her father's attention and affirmation were wrong; it's just that they were the exception, not the rule. When we live with so little love, we will grasp onto what we do receive in a way that becomes defining. Those moments may not reveal our true identity and calling, but they're all we've got.

We will draw our identity from outside ourselves; the question is, from whom? In the end, it will be from those moments and those people on whom we've had the biggest impact. Think again about Helen of Troy. Why "of Troy"? Wasn't she really Helen of Greece, Menelaus's wife? In calling her "Helen of Troy" we are forever reminded of the impact she had on the mediterranean world of the tenth century B.C. She is not Helen the Beauty or Helen Like No Other Woman. Those are qualities she could possess alone. No, she is Helen of Troy, which really means something like Helen the Fought Over, Helen the Captive and Rescued, Helen the Pursued. Her identity is inseparable from her relationships; it has been bestowed upon her. Maybe she enjoyed the attention, maybe not. Perhaps in the end she merely played the part of the rare art object, stolen from Menelaus's palace to be put on display in Troy. I hope that someone in all those thousands was pursuing her for her heart. But whatever else she felt, as the center of an international crisis Helen must have known beyond a shadow of a doubt that *she mattered.*

The gospel says that we, who are God's beloved, created a cosmic crisis. It says we, too, were stolen from our True Love and that he launched the greatest campaign in the history of the world to get us back. God created us for intimacy with him. When we turned our back on him he promised to come for us. He sent personal messengers; he used beauty and affliction to recapture our hearts. After all else failed, he conceived the most daring of plans. Under the cover of night he stole into the enemy's camp *incognito*, the Ancient of Days disguised as a newborn. The Incarnation, as Phil Yancey reminds us, was a daring raid into enemy territory. The whole world lay under the power of the evil one and we were held in the dungeons of darkness. God risked it all to rescue us. Why? What is it that he sees in us that causes him to act the jealous lover, to lay siege both on the kingdom of darkness and on our own idolatries as if on Troy—not to annihilate, but to win us once again for himself? This fierce intention, this reckless ambition that shoves all conventions aside, willing literally to move heaven and earth—what does he want from us?

We've been offered many explanations. From one religious camp we're told that what God wants is obedience, or sacrifice, or adherence to the right doctrines, or morality. Those are the answers offered by conservative churches. The more therapeutic churches suggest that no, God is after our contentment, or happiness, or self-actualization, or something else along those lines. He is concerned about all these things, of course, but they are not his primary concern. What he is after is *us*—our laughter, our tears, our dreams, our fears, our heart of hearts. Remember his lament in Isaiah, that though his people were performing all their duties, "their *hearts* are far from me" (29:13 *italics added*). How few of us truly believe this. We've never been wanted for our heart, our truest self, not really, not for long. The thought that God wants our heart seems too good to be true.

Craig, my closest friend, whom I've known for almost

twenty years, is a man I deeply respect. His life is full with many of the qualities I so want to reflect: insight, love, courage, a wonderful sense of odd humor, a man of sad gravity as the occasion requires. We live in separate states and our visits are rare and precious. As we were walking in the fields near my home one day, he was speaking about the future in a way that assumed we would be friends for life. Something stirred within me, and I heard my heart wonder, *Why would he want to be friends with me? What could he possibly see in me?* I was surprised by the honesty of my heart in response to being pursued, enjoyed. We just don't think there is anything desirable in us. And yet, we want to be desired. We were made for glory, for the attention that the Trinity gives to each other, and we can't live without it.

Things Are Not What They Seem

The reason we enjoy fairy tales—more than enjoy them—the reason we *identify with them* in some deep part of us is because they rest on two great truths: The hero really has a heart of gold and the beloved really possesses hidden beauty. In the last chapter, I hope you got a glimpse of God's good heart. But what about the second great truth—could we possess hidden greatness? It seems too good to be true.

Remember, the theme of veiled identity runs through all great stories. As Buechner reminds us, "Not only does evil come disguised in the world of the fairy tale but often good does too." The heroines and heroes capture our heart because we see long before they ever do their hidden beauty, courage, greatness. Cinderella, Sleeping Beauty, Snow White—they're not simple wenches after all. The beast and the frog—they're actually princes. Aladdin is "the diamond in the rough." If the narrative of the Scriptures teaches us anything, from the serpent in the Garden to the carpenter from Nazareth, it teaches us that things are rarely what they seem, that we shouldn't be fooled by appearances.

Your evaluation of your soul, which is drawn from a world filled with people still terribly confused about the nature of *their* souls, is probably wrong. As C. S. Lewis wrote in *The Weight of Glory*,

> It is a serious thing to live in a society of possible gods and goddesses, to remember that the dullest and most uninteresting person you talk to may one day be a creature which, if you saw it now, you would be strongly tempted to worship, or else a horror and a corruption such as you now meet, if at all, only in a nightmare. . . . There are no *ordinary* people. You have never talked to a mere mortal.

Imagine if Cinderella's story ended this way: "And the Prince married Grimheld, one of the brutish, wicked stepsisters, who complained about everything and picked her nose during the wedding." It's not far from our understanding of the gospel. The familiar refrain goes something like this: "You are a sinner, a traitor, a depraved wretch—pond scum, really. But God, in order to show the world what a great guy he is, will let you in anyway." We can't start with the Fall in our understanding of who we are and our role in the story. That's like coming into the movie twenty minutes late. But most Christian efforts to explain the story begin there. The whole idea of a fall assumes a starting place from which to plummet and given what a big deal the Bible makes of the Fall, it must have been from a pretty high place. "Boy trips, stubs toe" doesn't make the evening news. "Skydiver jumps, chute fails" does. The higher the original position, the bigger the story. Nobody's surprised when the neighborhood mutt runs off, plays the mongrel, sows a few wild oats, and kicks off a great night by rummaging through the trash. But what's the response if the Queen of England is found rolling around in the alley?

Yes, we are not what we were meant to be, and we know it.

If, when passing a stranger on the street, we happen to meet eyes, we quickly avert our glance. Cramped into the awkward community of an elevator, we search for something, anything to look at instead of each other. We sense that our real self is ruined, and we fear to be seen. But think for a moment about the millions of tourists who visit ancient sites like the Parthenon, the Colosseum, and the Pyramids. Though ravaged by time, the elements, and vandals through the ages, mere shadows of their former glory, these ruins still awe and inspire. Though fallen, their glory cannot be fully extinguished. There is something at once sad and grand about them. And such we are. Abused, neglected, vandalized, fallen—we are still fearful and wonderful. We are, as one theologian put it, "glorious ruins." But unlike those grand monuments, we who are Christ's have been redeemed and are being renewed as Paul said, "day by day," restored in the love of God.

Why is it that thousands of years later, Helen's story still has the power to haunt us? Isn't it that we long to believe beauty really could do that—there really might be someone worth launching a thousand ships to regain and someone willing, out of passionate love, to launch those ships? God has launched his ships for us. Could it be that we, all of us, the homecoming queens and quarterbacks and the passed over and picked on, really possess hidden greatness? Is there something in us worth fighting over? The fact that we don't see our own glory is part of the tragedy of the Fall; a sort of spiritual amnesia has taken all of us. Our souls were made to live in the Larger Story, but as Chesterton discovered, we have forgotten our part:

> We have all read in scientific books, and indeed, in all romances, the story of the man who has forgotten his name. This man walks about the streets and can see and appreciate everything; only he cannot remember who he is. Well, every man is that man in the story. Every man has forgotten who he is. . . . We are all under the

same mental calamity; we have all forgotten our names. We have all forgotten what we really are. (*Orthodoxy*)

Every woman is in some way searching for or running from her beauty and every man is looking for or avoiding his strength. Why? In some deep place within, we remember what we were made to be, we carry with us the memory of gods, image-bearers walking in the Garden. So why do we flee our essence? As hard as it may be for us to see our sin, it is far harder still for us to remember our glory. The pain of the memory of our former glory is so excruciating, we would rather stay in the pigsty than return to our true home. We are like Gomer, wife of the prophet Hosea, who preferred to live in an adulterous affair rather than be restored to her true love. Like Helen, we participated in our capture, though we were duped into it. And like Helen, our king has come for us, in spite of our unfaithfulness. If it is true that our identity comes from the impact we have on others, then our deepest and truest identity comes from the impact we've had on our most significant Other. Listen to the names he has given us: "No longer will they call you Deserted. . . . They will be called the Holy People, the Redeemed of the LORD; and you will be called Sought After" (Isa. 62:4, 12).

In other words, *we* are the ones to be called Fought Over, Captured and Rescued, Pursued. It seems remarkable, incredible, too good to be true. There really is something desirable within me, something the King of the universe has moved heaven and earth to get. George Herbert reached for words to express his wonder:

> "My God, what is a heart
> That thou shouldst it so eye and woo
> Powering upon it with all thy art
> As if thou hadst nothing else to do?" (*Mattens*)

King David used a similar refrain:

"What is man that you are mindful of him,
the son of man that you care for him?
You made him a little lower than the heavenly beings
and crowned him with glory and honor" *(Ps. 8:4–5)*.

The Scriptures employ a wide scale of metaphors to capture the many facets of our relationship with God. If you consider them in a sort of ascending order, there is a noticeable and breathtaking progression. Down near the bottom of the totem pole we are the clay and he the Potter. Moving up a notch, we are the sheep and he the Shepherd, which is a little better position on the food chain but hardly flattering; sheep don't have a reputation as the most graceful and intelligent creatures in the world. Moving upward, we are the servants of the Master, which at least lets us into the house, even if we have to wipe our feet, watch our manners, and not talk too much. Most Christians never get past this point, but the ladder of metaphors is about to make a swift ascent. God also calls us his children and himself our heavenly Father, which brings us into the possibility of real intimacy—love is not one of the things a vase and its craftsman share together, nor does a sheep truly know the heart of the shepherd, though it may enjoy the fruits of his kindness. Still, there is something missing even in the best parent-child relationship. Friendship levels the playing field in a way family never can, at least not until the kids have grown and left the house. Friendship opens a level of communion that a five-year-old doesn't know with his mother and father. And "friends" are what he calls us.

But there is still a higher and deeper level of intimacy and partnership awaiting us at the top of this metaphorical ascent. We are lovers. The courtship that began with a honeymoon in the Garden culminates in the wedding feast of the Lamb. "I will take delight in you," he says to us, "as a bridegroom rejoices over his bride, so will I rejoice over you," so that we might say in return, "I am my beloved's and his desire is for me."

Lady Julian of Norwich was given a series of revelations into the sufferings of Christ and the glory of the gospel. She was taken into the heart of God and upon her return she concluded quite simply, "We are his lovers." The bridal imagery often fails to capture a man's heart, but consider: God is neither male nor female. Both genders together are needed to reflect his image and he transcends them both. The question every woman is asking goes something like, "Am I lovely? Do you want me?" The question every man is asking is, "Do I have what it takes? Am I adequate?" As men and women, we want to be chosen for different reasons, but we both want to be chosen, to be welcomed into the heart of things, invited into the Drama to live from our heart. We both want love, the adventure of intimacy, and this is what God's pursuit means for men and for women.

> O Living Flame of Love . . .
> How Gently and how lovingly
> Thou wakest in my bosom,
> Where alone thou secretly dwellest;
> And in Thy sweet breathing
> Full of grace and glory,
> How tenderly Thou fillest me with Thy love.

These words, penned by St. John of the Cross in his book *Living Flame of Love*, capture the heart-cry of every soul for intimacy with God. For this we were created and for this we were rescued from sin and death. In Ephesians, Paul lets us in on a little secret: We've been more than noticed. God has pursued us from farther than space and longer ago than time. Our romance is far more ancient than the story of Helen of Troy. God has had us in mind since before the Foundations of the World. He loved us before the beginning of time, has come for us, and now calls us to journey toward him, with him, for the consummation of our love.

Who am I, really? The answer to that question is found in the answer to another: What is God's heart toward me, or, how do I affect him? If God is the Pursuer, the Ageless Romancer, the Lover, then there has to be a Beloved, one who is the Pursued. This is our role in the story.

In the end, all we've ever really wanted is to be loved. "Love comes from God," writes St. John. We don't have to get God to love us by doing something right—even loving him. "This is love: not that we loved God but that he loved us and sent his Son as an atoning sacrifice for our sins." Someone has noticed, someone has taken the initiative. There is nothing we need to do to keep it up, because his love for us is not based on what we've done, but who we are: His beloved. "I belong to my lover, and his desire is for me" (Song 7:10).

8

The Adversary: Legends of the Fall

The great snake lies ever half awake, at the bottom of the pit of the world, until he awakens in hunger.

T.S. Eliot

WE ARE THE SONS AND DAUGHTERS of God, even more, the Beloved, pursued by God himself. The images John has given us in the last two chapters do indeed, "take our breath away." We might think that, having our heart and mind bolstered by these images of beauty and truth, we would live our lives with courage and energy that arise out of the exuberant hope we have in the future. But there is another voice that whispers in our ear a very different message: a message in a minor and condemning key; a key that dilutes or even erases the truths John has portrayed so well. Some of this music in minor key we can ascribe to the pathos of living on this side of the Fall. Along with the creation itself, we will experience an inner groaning until Christ returns to wipe away every tear and establish his kingdom with us in joy and laughter.

But what is the source of the persistent accusations in our head and heart? It is a voice that speaks to us in tones and words vaguely familiar. The words and accusations that slide almost unnoticed into our consciousness are words we have heard before, sometimes from parents, peers, or the enemies of our youth. The voice (sometimes voices) that accuses us is so familiar we have learned to think of it as our own. Many of us have learned to use the voice to help us control life's unknowns—or so we think. It is a voice that constantly questions the wisdom of hope and the life of faith and love that flows from it.

It is the voice of our adversary.

Ezekiel gives us a portrait of this mortal enemy, before his revolt, in his prophecy against the king of Tyre, which is also a description of the angel that energized this king's heart:

> You were the model of perfection,
> full of wisdom and perfect in beauty.
> You were in Eden,
> the garden of God;
> every precious stone adorned you:
> ruby, topaz, and emerald,
> chrysolite, onyx and jasper,
> sapphire, turquoise and beryl.
> Your settings and mountings were made of gold;
> on the day you were created they were prepared.
> You were anointed as a guardian cherub,
> for so I ordained you.
> You were on the holy mount of God;
> you walked among the fiery stones.
> You were blameless in your ways
> from the day you were created
> till wickedness was found in you.
> Through your widespread trade
> you were filled with violence,
> and you sinned.
> *So I drove you in disgrace from the mount of God,*
> and I expelled you, O guardian cherub,
> from among the fiery stones.
> Your heart became proud
> on account of your beauty,
> and you corrupted your wisdom
> because of your splendor.
> So I threw you to the earth;

I made a spectacle of you before kings.
(Ezke. 28:12–17, italics mine)

The apostle John gives us, in more detail, the result of Lucifer's presumption:

And there was war in heaven. Michael and his angels fought against the dragon, and the dragon and his angels fought back. But he was not strong enough, and they lost their place in heaven. The great dragon was hurled down—that ancient serpent called the devil or Satan, *who leads the whole world astray. He was hurled to the earth, and his angels with him. (Rev. 12:7–9, italics mine)*

Our enemy is the angel Lucifer, son of the morning, one of the first and highest angels God created. He is the antagonist in the sacred romance—the great villain. All other villains are only a shadow of him. He is the one God gave a place of honor and trust "among the fiery stones" of the courts of heaven and who sees God face-to-face even to this day. He is one who spurned God's love and lost everything good through the sin of presumption. His desire was, and still is, to possess everything that belongs to God, including the worship of all those whom God loves. And God, as the Author of the great Story in which we are all living, has mysteriously allowed him a certain freedom to harass and oppress the other characters in the play, sometimes in a severe manner.

In some ways, due to his great age and dark wisdom, Satan knows us better than we know ourselves. The one purpose of his heart is the destruction of all that God loves, particularly his beloved. He stalks us day and night, as the Lord tells us through Peter: "Your enemy the devil prowls around like a roaring lion looking for someone to devour" (1 Peter 5:8). Peter makes it clear he is talking especially to believers, saying in verse 9, "Resist him, standing firm in the faith, because you know that *your brothers* throughout the world are undergoing the same kind of sufferings" (emphasis mine).

As I (Brent) read these words, several questions come immediately to mind, among them these: "Wait a minute, God. How did I get in the middle of this fight? Why do you give your enemy the freedom to attack me? And where am I to expect his attacks? A roaring lion should be fairly easy to identify. Where is this enemy of yours who is now also mine? What is his strategy to separate me from you and how does he carry it out?"

A Heart for Revenge

What is clear is that Satan has lost the battle. Twice. The first time he was hurled in disgrace from the walls of heaven by Christ and his angels. The second time, he was unable to hold the crucified Christ within the gates of hell and was forced to hand over to him the keys to death and Hades. But for a time he is placed on what feels like a very long leash to do what he can among us with his roaring.

As we pick up the drama of Satan's defeat in heaven at the end of Act II, which John described to us in Chapter 6 through Paradise Lost, we find Satan lying facedown in the lake of fire after having been hurled from the walls of heaven on the third day of his great battle with God and his angels. In shock that such a great force as his could have actually been defeated, he drags himself to a nearby island. He raises his head to see his angelic army strewn across the lake of fire like "autumn leaves"—the glow of heaven still upon them. Beelzebub, his chief lieutenant, convinces him to speak, that the sound of his voice might yet instill courage and hope in his legions.

Having lost everything with no chance for redemption, Lucifer, now Satan, tries to quiet the tears of his own heart and assure his legions that this place will never be able to hold such celestial spirits as they. He uses the despair, impotent rage, and hatred for God that they all feel to stir them to consider what "mature counsel" will once again give them hope and direction. Lucifer and his war chiefs have lost their heavenly names but Milton refers to them by the names their notoriety on the earth will earn them. Moloch urges all-out assault on heaven and if they die in the process, so be it. At least the streets of heaven will run red with blood. Belial, the consummate politician, advises a policy of laying low so that perhaps God will eventually forget about them and they can then do what they want. Mammon basically says, "Guys, we can own this joint without God here to bug us. We'll run a numbers racket never before seen under heaven." It is at this point that Beelzebub breaks in to the dialogue with exasperation:

> What sit we then projecting peace and war?
> War hath determin'd us and foil'd us with loss
> Irreparable; terms of peace, yet none
> Vouchsaf't or sought; for what peace will be giv'n
> To us enslav'd, but custody severe,
> And stripes, and arbitrary punishment . . .
> Nor will occasion want, nor shall we need
> With dangerous expedition to invade
> Heav'n, whose high walls fear no assault or Siege
> Or ambush from the Deep. What if we find
> some easier enterprise? . . .

Having expressed how futile it would be to place any hope in invading heaven or somehow pulling one over on God and establishing their own kingdom, Beelzebub advocates a different approach to gaining revenge against God by destroying or seducing God's new and favored race called man.

> There is a place
> (If ancient and prophetic fame in Heav'n
> Err not) another place, the happy seat
> Of some new Race call'd Man, about this time

To be created, like to us, though less
In power and excellence, but favour'd more
Of him who rules above; so was his will
Pronounc'd among the Gods, and by an Oath,
That shook Heav'n's whole circumference, confirm'd.
Thither let us bend all our thoughts, to learn
What creatures there inhabit, of what mould,
Or substance, how endu'd, and what their Power,
And whence their weakness, how attempted best,
By force or subtlety: Though Heav'n be shut,
And Heav'n's high Arbitrator sit secure
In his own strength, this place may lie expos'd
The utmost border of his Kingdom, left
To their defense who hold it: here perhaps
Some advantageous act may be achiev'd
By sudden onset, either with Hell fire
To waste his whole Creation, or possess
All as our own, and drive as we were driven,
The puny habitants, or if not drive,
Seduce them to our Party, that their God
May prove their foe, and with repenting hand
Abolish his own works. This would surpass
Common revenge, and interrupt his Joy
In our Confusion, and our Joy upraise
In his disturbance; when his darling Sons
Hurl'd headlong to partake with us, shall curse
Their frail Originals, and faded bliss,
Faded so soon. *(italics mine)*

Being unable to defeat God through raw power, Satan's legions decide to wound God as deeply as possible by stealing the love of his beloved through seduction. And having "seduced them to his party," to ravish them body and soul; and having ravished them, to mock them even as they are hurled to the depths of hell with God himself unable to save them because of their rejection of him. This is Satan's motivation and goal for every man, woman, and child into whom God ever breathed the breath of life. Like a roaring lion, he "hungers" for us.

God could have given up on the love affair with mankind. He could have resorted to power and demanded our loyalty, or given us a kind of spiritual lobotomy that would take away our choice to love him. Even now, he could easily obliterate our enemy and demand the allegiance of our hearts, but the love affair that began in the laughter of the Trinity would be over, at least for us. And Satan's accusation that the kingdom of God is established only through raw power would be vindicated.

Once we understand God's desire to possess our heart through love rather than power, we can fathom even more deeply the depths of God's anguish as he pleads with Israel through the prophets to give up their spiritual adultery and return to his love. We can also comprehend the fierceness of his jealousy for the heart and spiritual well-being of his chosen ones as he raises up nations and armies to obliterate the society and culture that have become a breeding ground for the enemy's seduction of their heart. "I do this so you will know that it is I Who am the Lord your God" is the heart message he brings to Israel in Ezekiel and Jeremiah. "And when you have been stripped naked and ravished, your hearts will again call out to me for rescue and I will come and destroy your enemies."

All of us have had poignant ecstasies of heart over a love affair that subsequently turned to immobilizing pain and shock as we realized that our lover could actually know us and yet leave us for another. But have you ever dated someone and you just knew, from the first time you met her, that she was the one you wanted to spend your life with? As you laughed and talked and marveled together, you felt your love deepen to a heart bond that you knew you never wanted to free yourself from. And have you ever been shocked to find one day that the one you loved so deeply and who you thought loved you just as passionately, had been dating other guys and, moreover, was spending more and more of her time with your worst enemy?

Have you ever had to literally turn a lover over to a mortal enemy to allow her to find out for herself what his intentions toward her really were? Have you ever had to lie in bed knowing she was believing his lies and was having sex with him every night? Have you ever sat helplessly by in a parking lot, while your enemy and his friends took turns raping your lover even as you sat nearby, unable to win her heart enough so she would trust you to rescue her? Have you ever called this one you had loved for so long, even the day after her rape, and asked her if she was ready to come back to you only to have her say her heart was still captured by your enemy? Have you ever watched your lover's beauty slowly diminish and fade in a haze of alcohol, drugs, occult practices, and infant sacrifice until she is no longer recognizable in body or soul? Have you ever loved one so much that you even send your only son to talk with her about your love for her, knowing that he will be killed by her? (And in spite of knowing all of this, he was willing to do it because he loved her, too, and believed you were meant for each other.)

All this and more God has endured because of his refusal to stop loving us. Indeed, the very depth and faithfulness of his love for us, along with his desire for our freely given love in return, are what give Satan the ammunition to wound God so deeply as he carries out his unceasing campaign to make us into God's enemy.

The journey of our individual hearts, as well as the heart of an entire nation or culture, really distills into this warfare for our heart's devotion. It is the central plot of the Sacred Romance, Act III, life here on earth. Indeed, all of the subplots of our lives come out of it. Satan has camouflaged this simplicity with a thousand other religions, psychologies, philosophies, knowledges, and mysticisms over the centuries, but the embers of the love affair, sustained by God's faithfulness, have refused to die and grow completely cold.

Satan's Grand Strategy

God and Satan each have a design, a battle plan, to capture our heart's devotion. The intimacy, beauty, and adventure of the Sacred Romance are placed and nurtured in the deepest longings of our heart by God himself. God's grand strategy, birthed in his grace toward us in Christ, and nurtured through the obedience of disciplined faith, is to release us into the redeemed life of our heart, knowing it will lead us back to him even as the North Star guides a ship across the vast unknown surface of the ocean.

If we were to find ourselves living with total freedom, Jesus informs us through his summary of the law in Luke 10:26–28, we would find ourselves loving God with all of our heart and our neighbors as ourselves. Jesus said further, "You will know the truth [me], and the truth will set you free."

The enemy knows this as well and his strategy to capture us is simply the opposite: to disconnect us from our heart and the heart of God toward us by any means possible. It is what he no doubt had to do to his own heart to bear the loss of heaven. Milton captures this terrible picture in earlier lines from *Paradise Lost* as Lucifer tries to speak to his fallen legions: "Thrice he assay'd [tried to speak], and thrice in spite of scorn, Tears such as angels weep burst forth. . . ."

Before Lucifer could become a true citizen of hell, he had to kill the desires of his own heart. He did it with scorn and much scorn was required. And this is his strategy with each of us: to kill the desire that would eventually lead us back to the One who loves us, using all the forms of shame, contempt, apathy, anesthesia, and perversion at his disposal.

The core of Satan's plan for each of us is not found in

tempting us with obvious sins like shoplifting or illicit sex. These things he uses more as maintenance strategies. His grand tactic in separating us from our heart is to sneak in as the Story-teller through our fears and the wounds we have received from life's Arrows. He weaves a story that becomes our particular "Message of the Arrows." Counting on our vanity and blind-ness, he seduces us to try to control life by living in the smaller stories we all construct to one degree or another. He accuses God to us and us to God. He accuses us through the words of parents and friends and God himself. He calls good evil and evil good and always helps us question whether God has anything good in mind in his plans for us. He steals our innocence as chil-dren and replaces it with a blind naïveté or cynicism as adults.

At the same time Satan is at work reinterpreting our own individual stories in order to make God our enemy, he is also at work dismantling the Sacred Romance—the Larger Story God is telling—so that there is nothing visible, as John wrote earlier, "to take our breath away." He separates beauty from truth and thus our thirst from our religious practice and the obedience of faith. He dismantles our church liturgical seasons that tell the story of a great love affair—of Paradise lost—and just when we believed everything to be hopeless—Paradise regained. He replaces the love affair with a religious system of do's and don'ts that parch our hearts and replaces our worship and communion services with entertainment. Our experience of life deteriorates from the passion of a grand love affair, in the midst of a life-and-death battle, to an endless series of chores and errands, a busy-ness that separates us from God, each other, and even from our own thirstiness.

"But can you really trust the thirst of your heart?" the enemy whispers in my ear. "Doesn't Jeremiah, God's own prophet, even say 'The heart is deceitful beyond all things and beyond cure'?" And the answer to that is, "Yes. Once my heart is sepa-rated from the life of the Sacred Romance, offered to me through the atonement of Christ, and left to seek out life on its own terms, there is no perversity it will not sink to." Part of Satan's grand strategy of separating us from our heart, once Jesus has drawn us to an awareness of being his sons and daughters through believing faith, is to convince us that our heart's desires are *at core* illegitimate. He comes in as the Storyteller and whispers to us: "Do you really think you are somebody special? Can you ever satisfy God's law without killing your heart and earning your keep? Do you think God really loves you beyond your usefulness? Hasn't your own experience taught you this is true?"

"Cinderella," the beloved fairy tale of our youth, captures wonderfully Satan's tactics as the Storyteller. As you remember, Cinderella lived with her stepsisters, a shrewish pair who made her sleep with the coal in the furnace room and had her convinced she would never be anything more than a maid. I remember thinking as I looked at the pictures of Cinderella in my child's storybook, "Doesn't she know how beautiful she is? Can't she see she is so different from her stepsisters both inside and out? Why doesn't she just look in the mirror?"

But the voices of the stepsisters were loud and Cinderella could only see in her mirror darkly. She continued to take their abuse and serve them right up until the invitation to the Prince's Ball came. When Cinderella shyly suggested that she might like to go, the stepsisters mock her to scorn for thinking she would fit in with people of such grace and beauty. As she helps stuff them into their costumes and does her best to hide their ludicrous ugliness, they continue to mock her foolishness in thinking that the prince would ever want anything to do with her. When God's grace comes in the form of Cinderella's fairy godmother and dresses her in a beautiful gown, she does finally look in the mirror and sees clearly her great beauty, but she believes it is all due to magic.

Of course, the prince recognizes her as the one he has been looking for all of his life. He spends the evening dancing with her, totally enraptured in her presence. As the clock strikes twelve, Cinderella fears being exposed for the homely housemaid she believes she is and runs from the room, losing a glass slipper in the process. Even though she still has the other glass slipper in her possession, she does not come forward when she hears the prince is searching the city for the one who can wear the dainty shoe.

Once again, the stepsisters' voices have convinced her that she is contemptible in soul and body, good only for the homeliest of tasks. Fortunately for Cinderella, the prince is a romantic who will not give up searching the city until he has found her, and they live happily ever after. And so it will be with us who are the beloved of the great Prince who is Jesus. It is this destiny that so enrages our enemy and makes him determined to destroy the love affair that he can never have a part in.

A Disguised Roar

Earlier in the chapter, I quoted Peter's warning that Satan is like a roaring lion, seeking whom he may devour, and asked where we are to look for the lion's roar. Satan lost his place in heaven because God and his angels were simply more powerful. As John explained earlier, it is the issue of whether God is really good that is not resolved, and this argument is still going on, at least in our sector of the cosmos. As Beelzebub said, "Drive them as we were driven, / The puny Habitants, or if not drive, / *Seduce them to our Party*, that their God may prove their foe."

Having lost the battle of power, both in being driven from heaven and in failing to hold Christ captive to death and hell, Satan's tactic in separating us from our heart until that day when he regains enough power to embody the Antichrist is to seduce us to his party by making us believe that it is God who is our enemy. It is as the Storyteller that he enters Act III of the play (the Creation and Fall) in the Garden of Eden, employing his strategy of deception until he can return to the raw power he would like to use. He comes to the man and the woman in the Garden with his roar disguised. He comes as one who is concerned with whether God really has their best interests at heart. He begins to test how well the man and the woman really know the story line God has revealed to them by asking a question: "He said to the woman, 'Did God really say, "You must not eat from any tree in the garden"?' The woman said to the serpent, 'We may eat fruit from the trees in the garden, but God did say, "You must not eat fruit from the tree that is in the middle of the garden, and you must not touch it, or you will die"'" (Gen. 3:1–3).

Contrary to the popular idea that Adam was not present at this point, possibly made so by Milton himself in *Paradise Lost*, Adam *was* present for this whole conversation, as is made clear in verse 6. God's original words to Adam were, "You are free to eat from any tree in the garden; but you must not eat from the tree of the knowledge of good and evil, for when you eat of it you will surely die" (Gen. 2:16–17). Eve adds the line, "[We] must not touch it, or [we] will die." She doesn't quite have the story straight, either because Adam had not made it clear to her or because she just didn't hear it with total accuracy. Either thought is somewhat incredible since this was before the Fall, but sin and evil always have a time of ripening before they bear their fruit.

Satan hears this flaw in Eve's lines and is emboldened to go further in his deception by directly contradicting the story line God gave to Adam. "'You will not surely die,' the serpent said to the woman. 'For God knows that when you eat of it your eyes will be opened, and you will be like God, knowing good and evil'" (Gen. 3:4–5). Satan's seduction of our heart *always* comes in the form of a story that offers us greater control through knowing good and evil rather than the unknowns of relationship.

The Cosmic Argument

And so it has gone ever since Adam lost his title as prince of the earth to the evil one. God, through the beauty of his creation, through the prophets, the Scriptures, and his Spirit who is in the world, and in those who believe through Christ, has continued to tell the story of his love for us, of what great beauty and significance we have in his eyes, along with his plans to bring us to intimacy with himself and all that is good. He exhorts us to trust in good in the midst of great evil. David Wilcox captures the poignant drama of this paradox God asks us to embrace in the lyrics to his song, "Show the Way":

> Look, if someone wrote a play just to glorify
> What's stronger than hate, would they not arrange the stage
> To look as if the hero came too late he's almost in defeat
> It's looking like the Evil side will win, so on the Edge
> Of every seat, from the moment that the whole thing begins
> It is . . .
> Love who makes the mortar
> And it's love who stacked these stones
> And it's love who made the stage here
> Although it looks like we're alone
> In this scene set in shadows
> Like the night is here to stay
> There is evil cast around us
> But it's love that wrote the play
> For in this darkness love can show the way.
> ("Show the Way," David Wilcox, © 1994 Irving Music, Inc., and Midnight Ocean Bonfire Music (BMI), All rights reserved. Used by permission. Warner Brothers Publications U.S., Inc., Miami, FL 33014)

Satan continues to use the evil that he himself creates to tell us a very different story. In his version, good is gained through our own understanding, not through a relationship with God. Life is gained by appropriating what we can see with our own eyes and by controlling any unknown Arrows that may strike us rather than living in the bigger Story God is telling. Jesus invites us to thirst. Satan invites us to control through performance of one kind or another.

His first goal, of course, is to make sure we never meet the Prince who is Jesus of Nazareth or experience a taste of the Great Ball. But once we have, Satan's second and lifelong purpose with each of us is to make sure we never know who we really are; indeed, to keep us living the life of a cellar maid rather than a princess. Even though we who are believers *have* tasted the Ball and the love of the Prince in beginning ways, the voices of the stepsisters continue to speak to us in tones varying from whispers to shouts; and like Cinderella, each of us has our own years as a "cellar maid" that the enemy can whisper to us about, causing us to wonder if this isn't who we really are after all.

The point is: We do not experience the story of our lives on rationally or emotionally neutral ground.

When I was young, I read a little book called *The Devil and Don Camillo*. It was the story of a Catholic priest whose heart was set to follow God. On one of his shoulders sat a small devil and on the other an angel, both of whom traveled with him wherever he went. As he encountered the events of each day, each spirit whispered intently in his ear its interpretation of the event and how it should be handled. This is perhaps as good an illustration of our situation as any I have come across. Satan's ministers constantly whisper to us their interpretation of the story of our lives in soul-specific ways. They use the events of our particular journey and bits and pieces of the lines spoken to us by parents, ministers, sweethearts, spouses, and perfect strangers. They weave these lines together into our particular Message of the Arrows that says there is no Sacred Romance, no larger Story that God is directing that is very good. They seduce us to the smaller stories of control and indulgence that so many of us find ourselves living, afraid to venture out any farther on the Christian journey. Satan is constantly at work deconstructing the Sacred Romance in our heart so that he may more easily seduce us to the smaller stories he is telling.

Given all this, it becomes crucial that we become a generation of storytellers who are both recapturing the glory and joy of the Sacred Romance even as we tell each other our particular stories, so that we can help each other, through God's Spirit, see his plan of redemption at work in us. In evangelical circles so often we try to apply formulas to each other with total disregard for where we are in our own story. For instance, there is a place on each of our journeys where we need to spend some time pursuing our emotions to see what heart-room they lead us to that may need tending. At other times, we need to acknowledge that a particular emotion is there but simply continue to live by faith. "You can't really study people," said C. S. Lewis, "you can only get to know them." We come to know God by coming to know the Sacred Romance he is telling. We come to understand who we are by telling each other our stories in light of the Sacred Romance.

Let me give an example of what I mean by "telling our story" from my own life. One of the deepest Arrows from my story has been the departure of three fathers, none of whom made any great effort to stay in contact or let me know that I was a significant loss. I mention this not to gain sympathy. Each of you who is reading these words has your own Arrows, some much worse than mine, others seemingly not as dramatic but perhaps even more poisonous due to their "invisibility." For instance, there is the daughter whose parents provide her every opportunity and meet every physical need, yet totally ignore her heart. I have talked about these things with my own father before he died as well as each of my stepfathers and we have reached a kind of peace that has allowed my Father in heaven to do much beginning healing. For some of us, that healing will come without the reconciliation with those who have harmed us. Nothing is impossible with God.

Having made these disclaimers, let me describe briefly how Satan, through his ministers, has woven these Arrows into a message in my life that has a very recognizable purpose for me as it does for you; it is to continue my life separated emotionally and spiritually from myself, my friends, and my family, as well as God my Father—*simply filling in time*. It is partly how my father ended his life, wandering from coffee shop to coffee shop and vacation to vacation, and to some extent, how my stepfathers struggled with theirs as well. They had no story powerful enough to sustain their waning years.

For my stepfathers, it was an end that did not appear totally unglamorous. They were both cowboys and cowboys wear aloneness with a certain heroism. It is their scripts that I have partially adopted. For other men, the script may be anesthesia or order or making money (for women, the script revolves around the heart issue of beauty or the avoidance of it)—whatever is sufficient to occupy the thirst of our heart enough that we don't need God.

My fathers' leavings gave the enemy a pernicious story line to work with; a stepsisters' message that his ministers have whispered in my ear constantly over the years. "You are on your own. There is no one to fall back on. You'd better figure out how to handle this. There's something wrong with you. Other fathers don't leave. It's all going to end badly. You're going to end up invisible and alone. Why don't you just give up this foolish idea that God cares and at least enjoy life in the ways you know you can."

Many of these thoughts have been with me from early on. They have been the energy that drove me to implement my own life script, making it up as I went along. They have been part of the energy that drove me to get a doctorate. They are even part of the energy driving me to write this book, though

I can confess that part of myself more easily than I used to. Those sentences are woven through and have partly energized the whole journey of my life. Thankfully, there are other sentences God has spoken into my life that are growing stronger even as the stepsisters' message dims.

Some of the sentences the enemy accuses each of us with have been there since we were young; others were added in the ensuing years as Satan saw opportunity to strengthen our fear and cynicism through "interpreting" those events in our lives that seem to verify our particular Message of the Arrows. His purpose is to convince us that we need to create a story to live in that is not as dangerous as the Sacred Romance. As long as we do not admit that the deep things of our heart are there— the rejection and hurt, the shame and sorrow, the anger and rage—these rooms of our heart become darkened and the enemy sets up shop there to accuse us.

I am not just speaking metaphorically or poetically when I refer to the enemy accusing us. Each of us, Christians included, is oppressed directly and specifically by the enemy in the way I am describing. This attack happens in the spiritual realm, using the sentences and voices we are familiar with from the past. We feel as if we are simply speaking to ourselves in our heads. And this is the enemy's first deception: "I am not here. It's just you struggling with all these things." Cinderella's stepsisters convinced her that it was her ugliness that brought her to her fate as a cellar maid rather than their harsh and condemning treatment of her. Many of us live our whole lives being defeated by this accusation. And indeed, deep in our hearts, the anxiety, shame, and self-contempt we often feel *are* like the attack of a roaring lion no matter what calmness or other personality device we learn to cover it with on the outside. We hide the lion's roar because he has convinced us that it is just us and we would be roundly scorned if we were to admit these things to others.

When the adversary is involved, the intensity of feelings

provoked by the everyday occurrences of life can be compared to gasoline poured on a fire. The fire would burn (i.e., we would hurt) even without the gasoline, but its additional fuel totally consumes the kindling of our souls in an inferno of shame and contempt. We feel ashamed for and contemptuous of ourselves as well as scornful of the people who have "caused" us such pain. They literally become our enemies that must be appeased or defeated. Meanwhile, the real enemy who caused this conflagration sits unnoticed in the background, full of glee. The whole experience is somewhat like being slapped in the back of the head in the school hallway. You turn around to find a boy next to you and slap him back, while the real culprit is already yards away enjoying the conflict he has instigated.

C. S. Lewis captures the destiny of the soul that Satan has in mind for each of us in his novel *The Great Divorce*. In the opening scene, we find ourselves at a bus stop in hell, from which we can see tiny pinpoints of light, each of which represents a dwelling. The bus stop is for those who might wish to travel to the outskirts of heaven and consider one last time if they would wish to be citizens there. Each dwelling visible to us is isolated from the others by darkness and great distance. From the different directions a few individuals move toward the bus stop, filled with great fear and ambivalence about leaving their familiar soul dwellings.

Lewis takes us to the window of one of these lone houses and invites us to look in. As we do so, we find Napoleon Bonaparte pacing back and forth muttering something to himself. As we listen more intently, we find him remembering his lost empire with great agitation: "It was Ney's fault. It was Josephine's fault. It was the Russians' fault." With horror, we realize that he is caught for all eternity in the failure of his particular small story, that of victorious and beloved emperor. Any of us who have spent any time rehashing how we were perceived at a party can relate to the torment of such a fate.

Satan uses the Arrows that strike all of us this side of the Fall, and weaves them into a story line to convince us that we cannot live without the disguise of our false self, the role we are playing out in what John and I have been calling our "smaller story." Our smaller stories are constructed along the plotlines of control and gratification. Once we begin to live by this false self, Satan and his minions sabotage the story to make sure we are exposed. Then he mocks us for our foolishness and hypocrisy for hiding behind such a facade in the first place. Other times, he simply leaves us to die in costume.

It has only been within the last five years that I have known that his script for me existed, and only in the last two that it has become increasingly clear how the enemy uses it tactically on a day-to-day basis. The seeds of the strategy are also visible in the other members of my family, seeds planted long ago to swell and bear bitter fruit in the right time. Each of our ancestral families also has a story that the enemy is busily reinterpreting according to that family's particular Arrows. (In this day and age, we have come to understand these things through the story line of psychology and genetics; e.g., the Joneses have always suffered with dependent personality disorder.) One theme in my own family line, for instance, is that of emotionally unprotected or neglected individuals marrying for safety rather than emotional intimacy.

It is not an issue of *whether* we are being assaulted by our particular Message of the Arrows, it is a matter of whether we recognize *how* our particular script reads. All of us are partly living out the story line the enemy offers us. This idea may seem too dramatic. Most of us, perhaps, live in not a terribly evil place in the moralistic sense of the word. We simply live where busyness, or apathy, or struggle with circumstances that won't change occupies most of our energy. And the enemy is perfectly happy to leave us in such a place practicing our religion. We are already defeated. The lion, if he roars at us at all, only does so internally about certain things we need to get under control or keep hidden with regard to the smaller stories we are counting on for life.

Spiritual Warfare and Deeper Communion with God

On the other hand, once we begin thinking of all the deceptions the enemy is about with regard to our lives, we have a tendency to become obsessed with him, fearful of what he is going to do next. Once we take him seriously, he switches from his tactic of "I'm not here" to one of having us worry about him day and night, which is almost a form of worship. God graciously showed me this several years ago while I was in the midst of an intense, three-year spiritual battle on behalf of a client who had spent years in the control of a satanic cult.

One night, David (not his real name) called me on the phone at three in the morning, in the midst of painful spiritual torment. We talked and prayed and I began to read from the Psalms. Finally, I could hear by his deep breathing that he had fallen asleep. As I lay on my dining room floor, pondering whether to leave the phone off the hook and build up a huge phone bill or hang up and risk having the beeping of the phone-off-the-hook signal wake David, something wonderful and strange took place.

In my heart, I heard a voice say, "Brent, forget about the battle. You're here with me now. Rest." I looked up, actually expecting to see God in some way, or perhaps an angel. What I did see was the light in the room *change*. I find myself wanting to say it grew more distinct, almost more personal. I only know I discovered that my hand was raised in the air in worship. I didn't decide to raise it. I am not, by any means, an expressive person in the charismatic sense of the word. It was simply as if there was no other appropriate response and my hand acted accordingly. For several minutes I basked in what I can only describe now as God's warmth and love toward me. The epiphany ended with me reading the Twenty-third Psalm and others it seemed the Lord had chosen to assure me that I was not alone in the battle.

From that night on, I had a whole new understanding of what both God our Father and the enemy of our souls are about once we leave behind the deception that Satan is not there and enter into the spiritual warfare that is part of the Sacred Romance, Act III. Again, Satan's desire is to keep us away from communion with God. He doesn't care how he does it.

God's intention, on the other hand, is to use spiritual warfare to draw us into deeper communion with himself. Satan's device is to isolate us and wear us out obsessing about what he has done and what he will do next. And he is very effective in using our particular Message of the Arrows to do it. God desires to use the enemy's attacks to remove the obstacles between ourselves and him, to reestablish our dependency on him as his sons and daughters in a much deeper way. Once we understand that, the warfare we are in begins to feel totally different. It is not really even about Satan anymore, but about communion with God and abiding in Jesus as the source of life. The whole experience begins to feel more like a devotional.

Through my own experience, I begin to see more clearly that God is so confident in the good that he is willing to allow our adversary latitude in carrying out his evil intentions for the purpose of deepening our communion with himself.

I do not mean to say this lightly. Sometimes there is a great cost to be paid in the establishing of the kingdom of God in our heart and in the heavenlies. The suffering and death of Jesus were required to bring about the life of the Resurrection. And Christ tells us through Paul that we are fellow sufferers with him. But the issue becomes more about our resolve to trust God's goodness than obsessing about the enemy's cloak-and-dagger warfare. The only reason to focus on what the adversary is doing at all is so that we can recognize the sentences of the stepsisters when we hear them and rebuke them with the truths of who we really are in the great Story God is telling. As we do so, we glorify God by trusting that his Story is the truth.

Indeed, part of God's victory over the enemy of our souls, which we will be invited to take part in, will be an open mocking of Satan and his forces in view of all the peoples of the earth along with the angelic hosts. We are given a picture of the enemy's defeat, which is the culmination of Act III of the Sacred Romance, by Isaiah:

> "Those who see you stare at you [Satan], they ponder your fate:
> 'Is this the man who shook the earth
> and made kingdoms tremble,
> the man who made the world a desert,
> who overthrew its cities and would not let his captives go home?'"
> *(14:16)*.

"You're the one we've been scared of all this time? You're the one we've been believing?" we will ask incredulously. And we will turn and walk away in the embrace of the Prince, never to speak Satan's name again. But in the meantime, our adversary will continue to use our Message of the Arrows, along with doubts about the goodness of the Prince, to lure us to spend our lives with less-wild lovers than God.

9

Less-Wild Lovers

*It is the nature of desire not to be satisfied, and most
human beings live only for the gratification of it.*

Aristotle

IN THE TIME of our innocence, we trusted in good
because we had not yet known evil. On this side of
Eden and our own experience of the Fall—whatever
our own Arrows have been and however the adversary has
woven them together into our particular Message of the
Arrows—it appears that we are left to find our way to trust in
good, having stared evil in the face.

Most of us remember the time of our innocence as a Haunting. I (Brent) mean innocence not as being sinless but as that
time before our experience with the Arrows crystallized into a
way of handling life which is the false self. The Haunting calls
to us unexpectedly in the melody and words of certain songs
that have become our "life music": the crooked smile of a
friend; the laughter of our children (or their tears); the calling
to mind of a mischievous face that still believed in joy; the smell
of a perfume; the reading of a poem; or the hearing of a story.
However the Haunting comes, it often brings with it a bitter-
sweet poignancy of ache, the sense that we stood at a crossroads
somewhere in the past and chose a turning that left some shining part of ourselves—perhaps the best part—behind, left it

behind with the passion of youthful love, or the calling of a heart vocation, or simply in the sigh of coming to terms with the mundane requirements of life.

Whenever I hear the old Frankie Avalon song "Venus," I see the blue eyes and dark hair of my first adolescent love, Kathleen. And I can feel the familiar Haunting seize my heart with palpable waves of longing and regret. We stood under the mistletoe together and I was afraid to kiss her. Even though our family moved to another state not long after, I thought for a long time it was that lost kiss that brought about the loss of the Sacred Romance; Romance that at sixteen is so embodied in first love. I felt there was something I could have done to hold on to the Sacred Romance by holding on to Kathleen.

And each of us has points of contact where the transcendence of the Romance has seared our heart in the fragrance of lovers, geographies, and times. They are captured there and return to haunt us with their loss whenever we return, or are returned, to their heart locale. At the end of the movie *A River Runs Through It*, the author, Norman MacLean, stands as an old man in the Montana river that defined the life of his family, now all gone. He casts for rising trout and something else. He tells us,

> Now nearly all those I loved and did not understand in my youth are dead, even Jesse [his wife]. But I still reach out to them . . . when I am alone in the half-light of the canyon, all existence seems to fade to a being with my soul and memories and the sounds of the Big Blackfoot River and a four count rhythm and the hope that a trout will rise. . . . I am haunted by waters.

My best friend experiences the Haunting whenever he reads the words of Robert Frost's poem "Nothing Gold Can Stay":

> Nature's first green is gold,
> Her hardest hue to hold.
> Her early leaf's a flower;

But only so an hour.
Then leaf subsides to leaf.
So Eden sank to grief,
So dawn goes down to day.
Nothing gold can stay.

The poem hangs on his office wall as a reminder of something lost.

Yet the people and times and places through which the Romance has seared us will betray us if we think that the Romance is *in* them, C. S. Lewis tells us:

> . . . it (is) not *in* them, it only comes through them and what (comes) through them (is) longing. . . . They are not the thing itself; they are only the scent of a flower we have not found, the echo of a tune we have not heard, news from a country we have never visited.

It is Lewis's way of telling us that the Romance is both set within us, and still out on the road ahead of us—a Haunting that calls us to pilgrimage.

At one time or another, though, most of us forget the Haunting, or try to; for it often threatens to cripple us, leaving us bent over and unable to deal with the everyday things that life requires to be done. We all, to some extent, take that shining something in us that felt magical and passionate as children, that something that later swirled amid the confusion of sexual passion and our longing for heart intimacy—we take it and push it through the loneliness, ache, and turmoil of life—through various stages of disconnection and hardness to another abiding place: a kind of resignation. There is something inside of us that says, "This is the way it is. I had better learn to deal with it." Thinking Act III, Scene 2 (the Fall) will go on forever, we lose heart.

In C. S. Lewis's science fiction novel, *Perelandra*, the story's protagonist, Ransom, is sent to the planet Venus to hinder Satan's attempts to seduce that planet's first woman, Tinidril.

He encounters her still in her innocence on the floating islands Lewis tells us cover the planet.

> Beautiful, naked, shameless, young—she was obviously a goddess: but then the face, the face so calm that it escaped insipidity by the very concentration of its mildness. . . . Never had Ransom seen a face so calm, and so unearthly, despite the full humanity of every feature. He decided afterwards that the unearthly quality was due to the complete absence of resignation, which mixes, in however slight a degree, with all terrestrial faces. This was a calm no storm had ever preceded.

Resignation is not just the sigh that groans with something gone wrong. Such a sigh can be redemptive if it does not let go of the Haunting we have all experienced of something presently lost. Resignation is the acceptance of the loss as final, even as I chose to interpret it on the bridge that long-ago November day. It is the condition in which we choose to see good as no longer startling in its beauty and boldness, but simply as "nice." Evil is no longer surprising; it is normal.

It is from this place of heart resignation where many of us, perhaps all of us at one time or another, having suffered under the storm of life's Arrows, give up on the Sacred Romance. But our heart will not totally forsake the intimacy and adventure we were made for and so we compromise. We both become, and take to ourselves, lovers that are less dangerous in their passion for life and the possible pain that comes with it—in short, lovers that are less wild.

Those of us who have been drawn to understand that God is our Father through conversion in Christ recapture the Romance again—for a while. We find ourselves again in the throes of first love. The Romance we thought we had left behind once more appears out on the road ahead of us as a possible destination. God is in his heaven and all seems right in the universe.

But this side of Eden, even relationship with God brings us

to a place where a deeper work in our heart is called for if we are to be able to continue our spiritual journey. It is in this desert experience of the heart, where we are stripped of the protective clothing of the roles we have played in our smaller stories, that the Message of the Arrows reasserts itself. Healing, repentance, and faith are called for in ways we have not known previously. At this place on our journey, we face a wide and deep chasm that refuses us passage through self-effort. And it is God's intention to use this place to eradicate the final heart walls and obstacles that separate us from him.

> I will go before you
> and will level the mountains;
> I will break down gates of bronze
> and cut through bars of iron.
> I will give you the treasures of darkness,
> riches stored in secret places,
> so that you may know that I am the LORD,
> the God of Israel, who summons you by name. *(Isa. 45:2–3 NIV)*

The Road Not Taken

God's imagery of going before us lets us know that he desires us to go on a journey. This is not so frightening. Most of us are aware that the Christian life requires a pilgrimage of some sort. We know we are sojourners. What we have sometimes not given much thought to is what kind of a journey we are to be taking.

"The line separating good and evil passes not through states, nor between political parties either—but right through every human heart," said Aleksandr Solzhenitsyn in the *Gulag Archipelago*. Not realizing it is a journey of the heart that is called for, we make a crucial mistake. We come to a place in our spiritual life where we hear God calling us. We know he is calling us to give up the less-wild lovers that have become so much a part of our identity, embrace our nakedness, and trust in his goodness.

As we stand at this intersection of God's calling, we look down two highways that appear to travel in very different directions. The first highway quickly takes a turn and disappears from our view. We cannot see clearly where it leads but there are ominous clouds in the near distance. It is hard to say if they hold rain, snow, or hail, or are still in the process of fermenting whatever soul weather they intend to unleash upon us. Standing still long enough to look down this road makes us aware of an anxiety inside, an anxiety that threatens to crystallize into unhealed pain and forgotten disappointment. We check our valise and find no up-to-date road map but only the torn and smudged parchment containing the scribbled anecdotes and travelers' warnings by a few who have traveled the way of the heart before us. They encourage us to follow them but their rambling journals give no real answers to our queries on how to navigate the highway.

"Each heart has its own turns and necessary overnights," they say. "Only God knows where your road leads. But come ahead. The journey is purifying and the destination is good." Faced with such mystery and irritating vagueness, we cast our glance down the other highway. It runs straight as far as we can see, with the first night's lodging visible in the appropriate distance. Each mile is carefully marked with signs that promise success on the leg of the journey immediately ahead if their directions are carefully followed. The crisp map we take from our valise assures us that heart baggage is not needed on this journey and would only be in the way.

As we turn to look at the old parchment one more time, our eyes find the sentences left by one former traveler, "Don't be afraid of embracing the disappointment you feel, old or new. Don't be scared of the unreasonable joy either. *They're* the highway markers home. I've gone on ahead. Yours Truly."

We snort with disdain at such quaint sentiments, and our choice made, we stuff the parchment into our valise and strike

off down the straight highway of discipline and duty. All goes
well for a while, sometimes for years, until we begin to realize
that we're really not feeling much anymore. We find ourselves
struggling to weep with those who weep or even rejoice with
those who rejoice. Mostly we don't bother looking people in
the eye. They may want to engage us and nothing much inside
feels very engaged. Our passions begin to show up in inappro-
priate fantasies and longings interspersed with depression, anx-
ieties, and anger we thought we had left behind. With a start,
we realize our heart has stolen away in the baggage. It is taking
the journey with us but under protest.

We redouble our efforts at discipline to get it to knuckle
under but it refuses. Some of us finally kill it well enough that
it no longer speaks as long as we're occupied. Any quasiredemp-
tive busyness will do. We look as if we're still believing. Others
of us decide the deadness is too high a price to pay and agree to
let our heart have a secret life on the side. We even try to be passionate about our faith but the fiery embers that once sustained
it have turned to cool gray ash, the evidence that life was indeed
once present.

"Two roads diverged in a yellow wood," wrote Robert Frost
in perhaps his most well-known poem, "The Road Not Taken":

"And sorry I could not travel both
And be one traveler, long I stood
And looked down one as long as I could
To where it bent in the undergrowth. . . ."

Ironically, having ignored the road that "bent in the undergrowth" and taken the more traveled highway of discipline and
duty, we find ourselves at the same place of heart resignation we
left so many years ago before we were Christians. We arrive at
the Vanity Fair that John Bunyan describes in *The Pilgrim's
Progress*. It is a familiar city populated with many of the com-
panions we had hoped to leave behind: deadness of spirit, lack

of loving-kindness, lust, pride, anger, and others. Nonetheless, having been out on the Christian journey for a number of years by now, we assume that this is as close to the Celestial City as we're ever going to get. We set up housekeeping and entertain ourselves as well as possible at the booths in the Fair that sell a variety of soul curiosities, games, and anesthetics.

The curiosities sold at the fair are endless in their diversity, many of them good in and of themselves: Bible study, community service, religious seminars, hobbies we try to convince ourselves are eternally transcendent (e.g., "Wow, I can't wait to ski deep powder!"), service to our church, going out to dinner. But we find ourselves doing them more and more to quiet the heart voice that tells us we have given up what is most important to us.

Life in Vanity Fair

Not even the most concrete of us live in a totally black-and-white world. Even so, we tend to fall into two groups when it comes to taking up housekeeping with these less-wild lovers— lovers who promise to deliver us from the Haunting of the Sacred Romance God has placed in our heart. Those of us in the first group choose anesthesia of the heart through some form of *competence* or *order*. These may be expressed in countless arenas: a clean desk, perfect housekeeping, Scripture memory and Bible study, a manicured lawn, a spotless garage, preparing and hostessing dinner parties that would make Martha Stewart proud, sending your boys to the best sports camps to ensure they (we) never experience disappointment that might provoke thirst, formulaic religion that has three-step solutions to every problem—the list is endless.

We don't stop to consider that the curse God announced to Adam and Eve dictates that we will never be under control, either in our vocations (we will not defeat the thorns and thistles of life), nor our relationships (Eve would desire to control Adam, but would fail). God's intentions here strike us as strange if not sadistic until we remember that Satan's offer to Eve was that she could bring about her own redemption through knowing good and evil.

If we were to try to picture the one who anesthetizes her heart to control life's Arrows as a wife, we would see a soul occupied by a seemingly redemptive busyness—involvement with her household and community that is productive and worthwhile. When her husband comes home from work, she is satisfied with a peck on the cheek and a few pleasant words about the day. She doesn't mind lovemaking if it's not too spontaneous but she rarely if ever pursues it. An evening of television or a good book would do just as well. Like Cinderella, she often settles into the lesser role of maid and housekeeper rather than risk rejection by wanting romance. Her husband will feel guilty—even accused—for wanting anything more with her. If he expresses his sadness over something lost in their love affair, she chides him for his melancholy spirit.

Sadness on this order, sadness about something they once had together but had lost, is what God was so often expressing to Israel (and to us) through the prophets. He was continually trying to invite her into a lovers' quarrel while she kept hearing his words on the level of an attack on how well she was performing her duties. One with an anesthetized heart hears God with Israel's ears.

The heart sentences of one who has taken on some form of anesthesia to tame her own heart as well as the heart of anyone who would want a romance with her, sound something like this: "My heart is not available for any love affair that requires engagement. I live only to avoid the surprises that the wildness of your desire, or mine, might bring. And if you were smart, you would do the same."

And underneath those brusque sentences is a person's story.

For some of us who have chosen anesthesia to tame our heart and the hearts of those who would love us, there is a hail of fierce and identifiable Arrows whose damage we try to contain by simply closing the door to the damaged heart places. For others of us, it was perhaps living in an atmosphere too fragile to bear the weight of our unedited souls. We grew up with a certain civility under which was an unadmitted demand that things be good. We learned that nothing considered "not nice" could be entered into without our world being in danger of shattering. Those around us let us know in no uncertain terms they needed us to be less-wild lovers. Sometimes whole cultures put this demand on us. Rosemary Daniell, in her book, *Fatal Flowers*, describes how the Southern culture she grew up in demanded that she literally divide her soul in two to be acceptable: a helpless Southern belle who was nonthreatening to men and Southern society, and a competent, independent career woman who could make up any family deficiency.

Our adversary also seduces us to abide in certain emotions that act as less-wild lovers, particularly shame, fear, lust, anger, and false guilt. They are emotions that "protect" us from the more dangerous feelings of grief, abandonment, disappointment, loneliness, and even joy and longing, that threaten to roam free in the wilder environs of the heart. These are feelings that frighten us, sometimes even long years into our Christian journey.

As I (Brent) write this chapter, Ginny and I are walking through a time in our marriage where we are trying to allow some of the sadness we both feel, due to years of misconnection and detachment in a certain area of our relationship, to be felt and expressed. Over the years, we have kept the feelings at bay with a bantering anger out of fear of where they might lead us (divorce?) if we admitted them. Having allowed ourselves to mourn, we both feel that there is a greater possibility of deeper romance in the years ahead.

If those of us in the first cadre of less-wild lovers choose to control our desire through various kinds of "stay-at-home" anesthesia, we who hang out in the emotional nightclubs of Vanity Fair choose a different kind of control: *indulgence*. We put our hope in meeting a lover who will give us some form of immediate gratification, some taste of transcendence that will place a drop of water on our parched tongue. This taste of transcendence, coming as it does from a nontranscendent source, whether that be an affair, a drug, an obsession with sports, pornography, or living off of our giftedness, has the same effect on our souls as crack cocaine. Because the gratification touches us in that heart-place made for transcendent communion, without itself being transcendent, it attaches itself to our desire with chains that render us captive.

A few years ago, I was counseling with a Christian man just ending a yearlong affair. He was married to an attractive and energetic woman who was also a believer, and he knew that he really loved her. He also began to understand that whatever it was that attracted him to the affair, it was not the woman herself, but something she represented. As we talked of making his break with her final, he wept with grief, immersed in the fear that some shining, more innocent part of himself would be left behind with the affair—left behind and, perhaps, lost forever.

And this is the power of addiction. Whatever the object of our addiction is, it attaches itself to our intense desire for eternal and intimate communion with God and each other in the midst of Paradise—the desire that Jesus himself placed in us before the beginning of the world. Nothing less than this kind of unfallen communion will ever satisfy our desire or allow it to drink freely without imprisoning it and us. Once we allow our heart to drink water from these less-than-eternal wells with the goal of finding the life we were made for, it overpowers our will, and becomes, as Jonathan Edwards said, "like a viper, hissing and spitting at God" and us if we try to restrain it.

"Nothing is less in power than the heart and far from commanding, we are forced to obey it," said Jean Rousseau. Our heart will carry us either to God or to addiction.

"Addiction is the most powerful psychic enemy of humanity's desire for God," says Gerald May in *Addiction and Grace*, which is no doubt why it is one of our adversary's favorite ways to imprison us. Once taken captive, trying to free ourselves through willpower is futile. Only God's Spirit himself can free us or even bring us to our senses.

If God's experience of being "married" to us, who are his Beloved, is sometimes that of being tied to a legalistic controller in the ways I've described in the paragraphs on anesthetizing our heart, at other times it is more like that of being married to a harlot whose heart is seduced from him by every scent on the evening breeze. In our psychological age, we have come to call our affairs "addictions," but God calls them "adultery." Listen again to his words to the Israelites through Jeremiah:

> "You are a swift she-camel
> running here and there, a wild donkey accustomed to the desert,
> sniffing the wind in her craving—
> in [your] heat [how can I] restrain [you]?
> Any males that pursue [you] need not tire themselves;
> at mating time they will find [you]
> Do not run until your feet are bare
> and your throat is dry" *(Jer. 2:23–25)*.

God is saying, "I love you and yet you betray me at the drop of a hat. I feel so much pain. Can't you see we're made for each other? I want you to come back to me." And Israel's answer, like that of any addict or adulterer, is: "It's no use! / I love foreign gods, / and I must go after them" (Jer. 2:25).

Perhaps we can empathize with the ache God experienced as Israel's "husband" (and ours when we are living indulgently). Having raised Israel from childhood to a woman of grace and beauty, he astonishingly cannot win her heart from her adulterous lovers. The living God of the universe cannot win the only one he loves, not due to any lack on his part, but because her heart is captured by her addictions, which is to say, her adulterous lovers.

Many of us have had the experience of not being able to bridge the distance between ourselves and others, whether they be parents, friends, or lovers. Whether the distance is caused by unhealed wounds or willful sin in our lover's heart—or our own—we experience their rejection as our not "being enough" to win them. Unlike God, we begin to think of ourselves as having a problem with self-esteem.

Whereas God became even more wild in his love for us by sending Jesus to die for our freedom, most of us choose to both become and take on lovers that are less wild. We give up desiring to be in a relationship of heroic proportions, where we risk rejection, and settle for being heroes and heroines in the smaller stories where we have learned we *can* "turn someone on" through our usefulness, cleverness, or beauty (or at least turn ourselves on with a momentary taste of transcendence).

The list of our adulterous indulgences is endless: There is the exotic dancer, the religious fanatic, the alcoholic, the adrenaline freak, the prostitute with a man, the man with a prostitute, the eloquent pastor who seduces with his words, and the woman who seduces with her body. There is the indulgent lover who never really indulges physically, but spends his life in a kind of whimsy about what is lost, like Ashley in *Gone with the Wind*. What these indulgent lovers have in common is the pursuit of transcendence through some gratification that is under their control.

In the religions of the Fertile Crescent, access to God (transcendence) was attempted through sexual intercourse with temple prostitutes. Perhaps, as we indulge our addictions, we are doing no less than prostituting ourselves and others in this very same way. "Every man who knocks on the door of a brothel is looking for God," said G. K. Chesterton.

At first glance, those of us who live by indulgence—illicit affairs of the heart—appear to have a certain passion that is superior to those who live by anesthesia. But it is a passion that must be fed by the worship or use of the other and so it is a passion that does not leave us free to love. Indulgence leaves us empty and primed for the next round of thirst quenching in an endless cycle that Solomon described as "vanity of vanities." Jimi Hendrix, one of our modern-day poets, just before his death of a drug overdose, said it this way: "There ain't no livin' left nowhere."

Life on that first road where the signs promised us life would work if we just applied the right formula—the road that seemed so straight and safe when we first set out on it—gives us no wisdom as to what we're to do with the depth of desire God has placed within us. It is desire that is meant to lead us to nothing less than communion with him. If we try to anesthetize it, we become relational islands, unavailable to those who need us; like the father who lowers his newspaper with annoyance at the family chaos going on around him, but makes no move to speak his life into it.

If we try to gain transcendence through indulgence, soon enough familiarity breeds contempt and we are driven to search for mystery elsewhere. So the man having an affair must have another and the man who is an alcoholic must drink more and more to find the window of feeling good. "There is only One Being who can satisfy the last aching abyss of the human heart, and that is the Lord Jesus Christ," said Oswald Chambers.

At the Edge of the Abyss

What, then, is the way of that less-traveled second road—the road that is the way of the heart?

We usually think of the middle years of the Christian life as a time of acquiring better habits and their accompanying virtues. But inviting Jesus into the "aching abyss" of our heart, perhaps has more to do with holding our heart hopefully in partial emptiness in a way that allows desire to be rekindled. "Discipline imposed from the outside eventually defeats when it is not matched by desire from within," said Dawson Trotman. There comes a place on our spiritual journey where renewed religious activity is of no use whatsoever. It is the place where God holds out his hand and asks us to give up our lovers and come and live with him in a much more personal way. It is the place of relational intimacy that Satan lured Adam and Eve away from so long ago in the Garden of Eden. We are both drawn to it and fear it. Part of us would rather return to Scripture memorization, or Bible study, or service—anything that would save us from the unknowns of walking with God. We are partly convinced our life is elsewhere. We are deceived.

"We are half-hearted creatures," says Lewis in *The Weight of Glory*, "fooling about with drink and sex and ambition [and religious effort] when infinite joy is offered us, like an ignorant child who wants to go on making mud pies in a slum because he cannot imagine what is meant by the offer of a holiday at the sea. We are far too easily pleased."

The desire God has placed within us is wild in its longing to pursue the One who is unknown. Its capacity and drive is so powerful that it can only be captured momentarily in moments of deep soul communion or sexual ecstasy. And when the moment has passed, we can only hold it as an ache, a haunting of quicksilver that flashes a remembrance of innocence known and lost and, if we have begun to pass into the life of the Beloved, a hope of ecstasies yet to come.

At some point on our Christian journey, we all stand at the edge of those geographies where our heart has been satisfied by less-wild lovers, whether they be those of competence and order or those of indulgence. If we listen to our heart again, perhaps for the first time in a while, it tells us how weary it is of the familiar and the indulgent.

We find ourselves once again at the intersection with the road that is the way of the heart. We look down it once more and see what appears to be a looming abyss between the lovers we have known and the mysterious call of Christ, which we now realize is coming from the other side. Jesus appears to be holding out his hand to us even as he calls us. He tells us he will provide a bridge over the chasm if we will abide in him. We hear his words, but such language is strange to us, sounding like the dialects of many who have used us or consumed us and then left us along the highway, exposed and alone. We pull back. Many of us return to Vanity Fair and mortgage our heart to purchase more of what is religiously or materially familiar.

A few of us arouse our spirit and take a step toward the chasm. We dig into our valise and pull out the old and torn parchment of road map and journal entries left by those who have traveled the way of the heart before us; the ones we had treated with such disdain. This time the words intrigue us. We realize they are telling us something about our heart that is true. One of them writes:

> Tis hard for us to rouse our spirits up—
> It is the human creative agony
> Though but to hold the heart an empty cup
> Or tighten on the team the rigid reign.
> Many will rather lie among the slain
> Than creep through narrow ways the light to gain—
> Than wake the will, and be born bitterly.
>   (George MacDonald, *Diary of an Old Soul*)

Yet, "holding our heart an empty cup" and "tightening on the team the rigid reign" is language we are not familiar with. Our lovers have so intertwined themselves with our identity that to give them up feels like personal death. Indeed, they have kept us from knowing the emptiness of our heart's cup. We wonder if it is possible to survive without them. We look once more at the journal to see if this sojourner ahead of us can offer any encouragement. He writes:

> But we who would be born again indeed,
> Must wake our souls unnumbered times a day
> And urge ourselves to life with holy greed.
> Now open our bosoms to the wind's free play,
> And now, with patience forceful, hard, lie still
> Submiss and ready to the making will,
> Athirst and empty, for God's breath to fill.

We are surprised and somewhat anxious at his words. We had expected him to give us religious instruction. Instead, he commands us to be greedy in our thirst, to open the windows of our heart to the "wind's free play." "What does this look like?" we ask.

"The answer is somewhat surprising," answers one who is standing at the chasm with us. "It is surprising because it happens in the context of everyday relationships and vocation." She tells us a story of how her own less-wild lover held her prisoner one day. She is a counselor, she says. Not long ago, two of her clients expressed their thankfulness for her help, saying she had done more for them in two sessions than previous counselors had done in months. Strangely, she found herself angry with them, admonishing them not to expect her to do "what they must do for themselves." As she reflected on her surprising anger, it became clear to her that she did not yet totally trust that she could live in freedom as a woman who was truly enjoyable. When her clients complimented her, her old less-wild lover of living by competence shouted at her that she had better keep coming across with counseling insights or her clients would no longer value her. It was how she had survived as a child and for a moment, she forgot the hope that God has placed something in her that is truly enjoyable, separate from her competence.

As she finishes her story, we puzzle over the truth that setting her heart free depends so deeply on trusting in her own beauty; on hoping in what is wildly good. We remember that the last line of the inscription on the gates of hell in Dante's *Inferno* reads, "Abandon all hope, ye who enter here." We pull out another of the old journals and read the apostle Peter's warning that our adversary is constantly at work (the lion seeking to devour us) to convince us that there is nothing wildly good, either in us, in God, or in his plans for the future of our love affair. "There is no such thing as true goodness," our adversary roars, "and if there is, it's deadly dull."

We wonder if it is our enemy who has convinced us that "good" is synonymous with "nice": the way we would be required to behave in Aunt Suzy's parlor on a warm summer afternoon when we would rather be swinging from a rope over the swimming hole.

It strikes us that to hope in the kind of goodness that would set our heart free, we must be willing to allow our desire to remain haunted. This side of the Fall, true goodness comes by surprise, the old writings tell us, enthralling us for a moment in heaven's time. They warn us it cannot be held. Something inside knows they are right, that if we could do so, we would set up temples to worship it and the Sacred Romance would become prostitution. We understand that we must allow our desire to haunt us like Indian summer, where the last lavish banquet of golds and yellows and reds stirs our deepest joy and sadness, even as they promise us they will return in the fragrance of spring.

Intrigued by these things and feeling the wind's free play on our face in a way we have almost forgotten, we seriously consider stepping out down the road we have so long feared and avoided. Just then our old lovers reach out for us with a vengeance. They promise us they will fill our heart to overflowing again if we will just give them one more chance. They even promise to become more religious if that will help.

Drawn by the familiar sound of their voices, and still somewhat anxious about the unknown journey ahead of us, we reach into our briefcase one last time to see if there is any solution to such double-mindedness. We find these words written by another traveler who also faced the chasm that has tortured and perplexed us so deeply. He assures us that even our deep ambivalence is part of the journey of the heart and that only severe measures by God himself can free us. He exhorts us to pray like this:

> Batter my heart, three personed God; for you
> As yet but knock, breathe, shine and seek to mend.
> That I may rise and stand, o'erthrow me and bend
> Your force, to break, blow, burn and make me new,
> I, like an usurped town, to another due,
> Labor to admit you, but, oh, to no end;
> Reason, your viceroy in me, me should defend;
> But is captive and proves weak or untrue.
>
> Yet dearly I love you and would be loved fain;
> But am betrothed unto your enemy;
> Divorce me, untie or break that knot again,
> Take me to you, imprison me, for I,
> Except you enthrall me, never shall be free,
> Nor ever chaste, except you ravish me.
> (John Donne, "Batter My Heart")

Partly afraid to pray for such bold movement from the wild God who loves us, we sit down to reflect on our plight. But this time, we are honest with ourselves. We admit that Vanity Fair really never *has* felt like home. We confess that we are truly captured by the less-wild lovers we have taken on, hoping that they would protect us from the Arrows even as they quenched our thirst. And we cannot deny, like it or not, that our lives have always been entwined with the characters in the Sacred Romance. We have lived under the hail of life's Arrows, some dragonlike in their ferocity, others—the everyday nits—small but continually troublesome. The Sacred Romance has touched us for a moment, but then has gone. It strikes us that we have nothing to lose. We get up and grip our valise for the unknown journey ahead of us. Something makes us search in it for an old scrap of paper. The words scrawled on it always bothered us when we came across them back in Vanity Fair. Now we read them for assurance:

> Two roads diverged in a wood, and I-
> I took the one less traveled by,
> And that has made all the difference.

We strike off down the road feeling much more alive than we have in a while. We are clueless as to how we will cross the abyss, but we feel a gladness to be on our way. Nonetheless, many questions nag at our consciousness as we walk. How are we to understand this journey which so few dare to travel? How are we to bring all of the characters and plots of the Sacred Romance together in our hearts and minds in a way that allows us to be transformed by the Story God is telling? Do we have all we need for the journey? Did we pack carefully enough to travel this more unknown road that is the way of the heart? Perhaps we should return home and get a few more things and a good night's rest before we undertake such a pilgrimage. All these things are on our heart as we begin.

10

On the Road

*But we who would be born again indeed, must wake
our souls unnumbered times a day.*

George MacDonald

EVERY GREAT STORY involves a quest. In J. R. R. Tolkien's *The Hobbit*, Bilbo Baggins ran from the door at a quarter till eleven without even so much as a pocket handkerchief and launched on an adventure that would change his life forever. Alice stepped through the looking glass into Wonderland; Lucy, Edmund, Susan, and Peter stumbled through the wardrobe into Narnia. Abraham left "his country, his people and his father's household" to follow the most outlandish sort of promise from a God he'd only just met, and he never came back. Jacob and his sons went to Egypt for some groceries and four hundred years later the Israel nation pulled up stakes and headed for home. Peter, Andrew, James, and John all turned on a dime one day to follow the Master, their fishing nets heaped in wet piles behind them. The Sacred Romance involves for every soul a journey of heroic proportions. And while it may require for some a change of geography, for every soul it means a journey of the heart.

In *Pilgrim's Progress*, John Bunyan's seventeenth-century allegory of the Sacred Romance, there is a man who comes to see his own story as he has never seen it before, and he is appalled by what he sees. He longs for life, real life, which is to say, eternal life, and he knows that to stay where he is means death. He has no more sense of direction than that he must go and find the path that leads to the Celestial City, his heart's true home. Against the protestations of family and friends, in rejection of all the comforts of his smaller story, he launches on a remarkable adventure: "So I saw in my dream" Bunyan wrote, "that the man began to run." A good place to start. But as Bunyan tells it, "he had not run far from his own door" before the characters in his small story ran to fetch him back, crying out all the threats and excuses they could think of. "But the man put his fingers in his ears, and ran on, crying, 'Life! life! eternal life!'"

This man becomes Pilgrim and the story of his journey is the story of our own. Entering into the Sacred Romance begins with a decision to become a pilgrim of the heart. As Gabriel Marcel reminds us, the soul is a traveler: "It is of the soul and of the soul alone that we can say with supreme truth that 'being' necessarily means 'being on the way' (*en route*)." We are, he says, "*homo viator*," which means "itinerant man," man or woman on pilgrimage. The choice before us now is to journey or to homestead, to live like Abraham the friend of God, or like Robinson Crusoe, the lost soul cobbling together some sort of existence with whatever he can salvage from the wreckage of the world. Crusoe was no pilgrim; he was a survivor, hunkered down for the duration. He lived in a very, very small world where he was the lead character and all else found its focus in him. Of course, to be fair, Crusoe was stranded on an island with little hope of rescue. We *have* been rescued, but still the choice is ours to stay in our small stories, clutching our household gods and false lovers, or to run in search of life.

Eyes for the Romance

We've gone from a creek side in New Jersey to the Cosmic Drama begun before the foundations of the world. We've met the main players in the Sacred Romance and gotten to know something of their true identities, their motives, and their roles in the story. Let's come back now to the daily grind of our own experience to answer the question, "What does all this look like in real life?" How is God wooing us through flat tires, bounced checks, and rained-out picnics? What is he after as we face cancer, sexual struggles, and abandonment? Does knowing that we are his Beloved make any difference at all? Would recognizing Satan's temptations and our less-wild lovers help us to live as freer men and women? What difference does all this make, anyhow?

The short answer is, it gives us *a way of seeing that reveals life for the romantic journey it truly is.*

Entering into the Sacred Romance begins with eyes to see and ears to hear. Where would we be today if Eve had looked at the serpent with different eyes, if she had seen at once that the beautiful creature with the charming voice and the reasonable proposition was in fact a fallen angel bent on the annihilation of the human race? Failure to see things as they truly are resulted in unspeakable tragedy. From that point on, the theme of blindness runs throughout Scripture. It's not merely a matter of failing to recognize temptation when we meet it; like Elisha's servant, we often fail to see the drama of redemption as well. As prophet to Israel, Elisha proved to be a major military liability for the Aramaeans. Every time these enemies of Israel planned an ambush, the man of God spoiled their fun by betraying their position to the otherwise unsuspecting people of God. Furious, the king of Aram decided to take out Israel's "radar" by killing Elisha. He learned where the prophet was holed up and sent an army to surround the city. The drama unfolds through the eyes of Elisha's servant:

> When the servant of the man of God got up and went out early the next morning, an army with horses and chariots had

surrounded the city. "Oh, my lord, what shall we do?" the servant asked.

"Don't be afraid," the prophet answered. "Those who are with us are more than those who are with them."

And Elisha prayed, "O LORD, open his eyes so he may see." Then the LORD opened the servant's eyes, and he looked and saw the hills full of horses and chariots of fire all around Elisha. *(2 Kings 6:15–17)*

Needless to say, Elisha's servant suddenly saw from a whole different perspective. I (John) think it's safe to assume he also experienced a bit of emotional relief—a recovery of heart. What for him had undoubtedly been a harrowing encounter became an exciting adventure.

The apostle Paul experienced an even greater surprise on the road to Damascus. Thinking he was doing God a favor, he was hell-bent on crushing a tiny religious movement called the Way. But he had the plot and the characters completely confused. Paul, known at that time as Saul, was playing the role of Defender of the Faith, when in fact he was Persecutor of Christ. It took a bout of blindness to bring things into focus, and when the scales fell from his eyes he never saw things the same way again. Paul later explained to the Romans that human sin and suffering are the result of foolish and darkened hearts, brought on by a refusal to see the Sacred Romance. It should come as no surprise that his most fervent prayer for the saints was that the scales would fall from the eyes of our heart so that we might not miss the Sacred Romance (Eph. 1:18–19).

Several years ago I went through one of the most painful trials of my professional life. The story involves a colleague whom I will call Dave, a man I hired and with whom I had labored several years in ministry. We spent many hours on the road together, speaking to churches about the Christian life. A point came when I needed to confront Dave about some issues in his life that were hurting his own ministry and the larger purposes of our team. In all fairness, I think I handled it poorly, but I was totally unprepared for what happened next. Dave turned on me with the ferocity of a cornered animal. He fabricated lies and spread rumors in an attempt to destroy my career. His actions were so out of proportion it was hard to believe we were reacting to the same events. He went to the head pastor in an attempt to have me dismissed. The attempt failed, but our friendship was lost and several others were hurt in the process.

In the midst of the crisis, I spoke with Brent one afternoon about the turn of events and the awful pain of betrayal. He said "I wonder what God is up to in all this?"

"God?" I said. "What's *he* got to do with it?" My practical agnosticism was revealed. I was caught up in the sociodrama, the smaller story, completely blind to the true story at that point in my life. Brent's question arrested my attention and brought it to a higher level. In fact, the process of our sanctification, our journey, rests entirely on our ability to see life from the basis of that question. As the poet William Blake warned long ago, "Life's dim window of the soul distorts the heavens from pole to pole, and leads you to believe a lie, when you see with, not through, the eye."

Allow me, then, to review what we have encountered. First, our lives are not a random series of events; they tell a Story that has meaning. We aren't in a movie we've arrived at twenty minutes late; we are in a Sacred Romance. There really is something wonderful that draws our heart; we are being wooed. But there is also something fearful. We face an enemy with vile intentions. Is anyone in charge? Someone strong and kind who notices us? At some point we have all answered that question "no" and gone on to live in a smaller story. But the answer is "*yes*"—there is someone strong and kind who notices us. Our Story is written by God who is more than author, he is the romantic lead in our personal dramas. He created us for himself and now he is moving heaven and earth to restore us to his side. His wooing

seems wild because he seeks to free our heart from the attachments and addictions we've chosen, thanks to the Arrows we've
known.

And we—who are we, really? We are not pond scum, nor are
we the lead in the story. We are the Beloved; our hearts are the
most important thing about us and our desire is wild because it
is made for a wild God. We are the Beloved, and we are
addicted. We've either given our heart to other lovers and can't
get out of the relationships, or we've tried our best to kill desire
(often with the help of others) and live lives of safe, orderly control. Either way, we play into the hands of the one who hates us.
Satan is the mortal enemy of God and therefore ours as well,
who comes with offers of less-wild lovers, hoping to deceive us
in order to destroy our heart and thus prevent our salvation or
cripple our sanctification. These are the stage, the characters,
and the plot in the broadest possible terms. Where do we go
from here?

Setting Out

We are faced with a decision that grows with urgency each passing day: Will we leave our small stories behind and venture forth
to follow our Beloved into the Sacred Romance? The choice to
become a pilgrim of the heart can happen any day and we can
begin our journey from any place. We are here, the time is now,
and the Romance is always unfolding. The choice before us is
not to make it happen. As Chesterton said, "An adventure is, by
its nature, a thing that comes to us. It is a thing that chooses
us, not a thing that we choose." Lucy wasn't looking for Narnia when she found it on the other side of the wardrobe; in a
way, it found her. Abraham wasn't wandering about looking
for the one true God; he showed up with an extraordinary invitation. But having had their encounters, both could have chosen otherwise. Lucy could have shut the wardrobe door and

never mentioned what had happened there. Abraham could have opted for life in Haran. The choice before us is a choice to *enter in*.

So much of the journey forward involves a letting go of all that once brought us life. We turn away from the familiar abiding places of the heart, the false selves we have lived out, the strengths we have used to make a place for ourselves and all our false loves, and we venture forth in our hearts to trace the steps of the One who said, "Follow me." In a way, it means that we stop *pretending*: that life is better than it is, that we are happier than we are, that the false selves we present to the world are really us. We respond to the Haunting, the wooing, the longing for another life. Pilgrim begins his adventure toward redemption with a twofold turning: a turning *away* from attachment and a turning *toward* desire. He wanted life and so he stuck his fingers in his ears and ran like a madman ("a fool," to use Paul's term) in search of it. The freedom of heart needed to journey comes in the form of detachment. As Gerald May writes in *Addiction and Grace*,

> *Detachment* is the word used in spiritual traditions to describe freedom of desire. Not freedom *from* desire, but freedom *of* desire. . . . An authentic spiritual understanding of detachment devalues neither desire nor the objects of desire. Instead, it "aims at correcting one's own anxious grasping in order to free oneself for committed relationship to God." According to Meister Eckhart, detachment "enkindles the heart, awakens the spirit, stimulates our longings, and shows us where God is."

With an awakened heart, we turn and face the road ahead, knowing that no one can take the trip for us, nor can anyone plan our way. When he sets out, Bunyan's Pilgrim has no map, no itinerary, no step-by-step travelogue with each day's adventure carefully planned out. All he has is his desire and a general idea that the way of life lies somewhere along the road ahead. As the poet Wallace Stevens wrote, "The way through the world is more difficult to find than the way beyond it." So many of the programs of modern Christianity with three steps to this and seven steps to that and a principle for everything are in fact an effort not to journey at all. More often than not, they are pursued with a desire to hunker down and make life work, here, now. The Sacred Romance is not something to be managed, but to be lived. We cannot remove the element of mystery from the road before us nor can we eliminate the dangers. But we can learn from pilgrims who have gone before something of the road conditions, the weather, the hazards, and the places of rest and refreshment.

On the Road: Dragons and Nits

Life, said Woody Allen, is divided between the horrible and the miserable. A cynical assessment, perhaps, but if we're honest we'll have to admit our journey is hardly along the primrose path. Pretending that life is easier and more blessed than it really is hinders our ability to walk with God and share him with others. Faith is not the same thing as denial. Blessings come, to be sure. But they tend to be infrequent, unpredictable, and transient. In the day-to-day pattern of things, our journey is shaped more often by *dragons* and *nits*—crises that shake us to the core and persistent troubles that threaten to nag us to death. Dragons and nits: Are they tragic events and random inconveniences, or are they part of the plot through which God redeems our heart in very personal ways?

Mary is a good friend of mine who lost her permanent front teeth through an accident in early adolescence. Years later, she struggled to finally resolve the issue with dental caps. What should have been a simple procedure took weeks, then months. Appointment after appointment, the caps were either the wrong color, the wrong shape, or the wrong size. When she finally did get a pair that she could live with, the glue didn't hold. Where was the Sacred Romance in such a mundane and yet withering struggle? Why didn't God ride in as hero and provide a beautiful set of caps? Wouldn't that have been the loving thing to do? As the ordeal continued, a major issue of her heart surfaced. Mary's teeth had long been for her a symbol of her struggle with the question of her inner beauty. Her teeth were a source of shameful arrows lodged deep. A seemingly irrelevant nit that God refused to take away became an opportunity to face a fundamental question the heart of every woman asks: Am I lovely? Without the nit, the deeper issue of her heart would never have come up. Once it did, the real battle began.

The Accuser stepped in with a subtle, deadly stream of thoughts: "Look, just settle for the wrong caps and get on with your life. Your desire for beauty is nothing more than vanity. Things will never change. God doesn't care for your heart or he would have taken care of your teeth." And finally, "This is who you really are: unlovely and unlovable."

Each time Mary looked in the mirror, these sentences urged her to lose heart. Some days, the crisis felt as if it would crush her spirit; on other days, she just felt dumb. Meanwhile, Mary's false lovers took their cue and began offering to help her deal with the pain. Food promised to take away her heartache; busyness lured her to bury it beneath a deluge of Christian service. Even the faith practiced by the charismatic church she attends offered to lift her beyond the struggle if she would only focus on the Lord and worship more frequently.

Thankfully, her True Love was persistent in his pursuit of her heart, refusing to let her take the easy way out. The question of her inner beauty broke to the surface one day, and, fortunately, a friend with eyes for the Romance was there to help her see what was at stake. Once Mary finally turned and faced the core issue, God was able to speak words of loving reassurance: "You are lovely, Mary, and I want you to offer your inner beauty, your womanly heart to the world." Through a seemingly insignificant and unspiritual issue like dental caps, God spoke healing to Mary's heart and invited her up into the Sacred Romance.

If we'll take time to reflect, the nits of our lives and the way we typically respond to them both have a *theme*, a pattern that reveals something important about our heart, something God is after. Mary's theme was the suppression of her beauty under "more spiritual distractions." Satan tempts us toward cynicism, resignation, and an offer of a safer or even a more exciting life if we will simply renounce our True Love and follow him.

The dragons are far more dramatic. The doctor announces he's found a lump; your spouse announces she is no longer in love with you. They are dragons because they strike at the core of our deepest fears. This is the dark night of the soul, when we face the implications of Job's question: *God could stop this. Why doesn't he?* Satan leaps in with a reaffirmation of the first temptation: "God isn't really your kind advocate after all." We're faced with a choice to fall back, clutch up, seize control, or enter more deeply into our lives and our beliefs and release more thoroughly to the love of God.

The Sentences We Live By

I'll never have the love I want. The sentence rose up from some deep place within me as I lay in bed one morning, looking for a reason to get up. My wife, Stasi, and I had been going through one of the hardest times we'd ever encountered in our marriage. Some days we both wondered if we would even make it; other days we wondered if we even wanted to. The wounds were too deep, the barriers too high; it just didn't seem worth the effort. Divorce seemed like a perfectly reasonable way out.

Beneath the anger and the disappointment lurked a far more defining issue of my heart. Years ago, when my father checked out of my life into alcoholism, an Arrow lodged deep within: *You are on your own.* In order to control that Arrow I made a resolution in my heart: *I won't need anyone, not deeply. I can make it without love.* But as the years rolled by, my heart refused to live in my self-created isolation. I looked for someone to fill the void in my life left by my father. I chose Stasi as the lucky girl. Beneath the stated marriage vows of "for better or for worse," what I was really saying was, "Stasi, I'm going to give you the opportunity of a lifetime. No one has ever really loved me the way I so desperately want to be loved, but I'm going to give you that chance. It lies in your power to validate my soul."

The pressure is more than any human being can bear. Even if she were a perfect woman, Stasi could never come through. But like all of us, she came into marriage with a set of demons all her own. Though she didn't face something as awful as alcoholism, her struggles seemed to me a terrible repeat of my father's because I felt the effect to be the same: I felt alone. Smelling blood, Satan closed in like a shark with suggestions like, "You don't have to put up with this, you know. There are options, other women. Besides, things will never change with Stasi." I turned to my false loves, losing myself in my career and spending my free time escaping through fly-fishing. I prayed that God would simply take away the trials in our marriage, but he didn't. I tried to live beyond my longing to be loved, but I couldn't. The stakes were incredibly high: a loss of heart, of our marriage, and the perpetuation of the family curse onto our boys.

There, in the wee hours of the morning, when our heart has the chance to catch us with its most honest thoughts, the sentence rose from the depths of my soul: *I'll never have the love I want.* The aching wound from years before was present to me again. And there God was able to begin to waken me to the Romance. Browsing through Scripture I read 1 John 4:7, a simple sentence, one I had probably read a thousand times before: "Love comes from God." It brought more hope than I had ever known. It spoke to the wound because the wound was awakened and I was ready to hear. As the weeks progressed, I embraced my longing to be loved and turned the validation of my soul over to my Father in heaven. Sometime later, while on a business flight to the West Coast, I was thinking about love and those words from 1 John. A new sentence arose in my heart: *I have the love I wanted all my life.*

Both dragons and nits take us into the deep places of the soul, uncovering the sentences we have long lived by. It was in the depths of his personal tragedies that Job uttered the ruling sentence of his heart: "What I feared has come upon me" (3:25). In other words, "I knew it! I knew I couldn't really trust God—not with the things that matter most." Job's idol was control and God was determined to save him from it. When the nits and dragons come, we ask God to remove them and when he doesn't, we take charge of our own well-being since it appears no one else will. The dragons and nits reveal to us (and to our community) where our attachments and addictions lie. In other words, they reveal where our heart is, other than captured by the love of God.

But there is more. Life on the road takes us into our heart, for *only when we are present in the deep sentences can God speak to them.* That's why the story is a journey; it has to be lived, it cannot simply be talked about. When we face trials, our most common reaction is to ask God, "Why won't you relieve us?" And when he doesn't, we resignedly ask, "What do you want me to do?" Now we have a new question: "Where is the Romance headed?"

There is another great "revealing" in our life on the road. We run our race, we travel our journey, in the words of Hebrews, before "a great cloud of witnesses" (12:1). When we face a decision to fall back or press on, the whole universe holds its breath—angels, demons, our friends and foes, and the Trinity itself—watching with bated breath to see what we will do. We are still in the drama of Act III and the heart of God is still on trial. The question that lingers from the fall of Satan and the fall of man remains: Will anyone trust the great heart of the Father, or will we shrink back in faithless fear?

As we grow into the love of God and the freedom of our own hearts, we grow in our ability to cast our vote on behalf of God. Our acts of love and sacrifice, the little decisions to leave our false loves behind and the great struggles of our heart reveal to the world our true identity: We really are the sons and daughters of God.

What to Bring Along

In her essay *An Expedition to the Pole*, Annie Dillard describes the provision carried along by nineteenth-century explorers in their search for the North Pole:

> Each sailing vessel carried an auxiliary steam engine and a twelve-day supply of coal for the entire projected two or three years' voyage. Instead of additional coal . . . each ship made room for a 1,200-volume library, "a hand-organ playing fifty tunes," china place settings for officers and men, cut-glass wine goblets, and sterling silver flatware. . . . The expedition carried no special clothing for the Arctic, only the uniforms of Her Majesty's Navy.

Years later, Inuit eskimos came across frozen remains of the expedition, men dressed in their finery and pulling a lifeboat laden with place settings of sterling silver and some chocolate. Their naïveté is almost beyond comprehension, but perhaps it will motivate us to be better outfitted for our own journey. What does one take on an expedition of the heart? What do we need to be prepared for?

Our journey begins with desire, "not for a raise," says poet David Whyte, "but for another life." Desire sets us on our way, yet what will keep desire alive? Enemies of desire lurk all along the way—fear, self-contempt, disappointment—these and a hundred other demons of the road are enough to extinguish the flame of the heart. Hamlet, that famous Prince of Denmark, gave poetic expression to the dilemma we all face: Why press on when there is little to look forward to?

> Who would fardels [burdens] bear,
> To grunt and sweat under a weary life,
> But that the dread of something after death,
> The undiscovered country, from whose bourn
> No traveller returns, puzzles the will,
> And makes us rather bear those ills we have
> Than fly to others that we know not of?
> 　(*Act III, Scene I*)

In other words, it's better to stay in the safety of the camp than venture forth on a wing and a prayer. Who knows what dangers lie ahead? This was the counsel of the ten faithless spies sent in to have a look at the Promised Land when the Jews came out of Egypt. Only two of the twelve, Joshua and Caleb, saw things differently. Their hearts were captured by a vision of what might be and they urged the people to press on. But their voices were drowned by the fears of the other ten spies and Israel wandered for another forty years. Without the anticipation of better things ahead, we will have no heart for the journey.

One of the most poisonous of all Satan's whispers is simply, "Things will never change." That lie kills expectation, trapping our heart forever in the present. To keep desire alive and flourishing, we must renew our vision for what lies ahead. Things will not always be like this. Jesus has promised to "make all things new." Eye has not seen, ear has not heard all that God has in store for his lovers, which does not mean "we have no clue so don't even try to imagine," but rather, *you cannot out-dream God*. Desire is kept alive by imagination, the antidote to resignation. We will need imagination, which is to say, we will need *hope*. I will say more about this in Chapter 12.

Well into his journey toward the Celestial City, Pilgrim

grows impatient with his progress. He leaves the narrow path for what he believes will be a shortcut, but is captured by the Giant Despair and held in the dungeon of Doubting Castle. Under the harsh treatment of Despair, Christian loses heart nearly to the point of taking his own life.

Julia Gatta describes impatience, discouragement, and despair as the "noonday demons" most apt to beset the seasoned traveler. As the road grows long we grow weary; impatience and discouragement tempt us to forsake the way for some easier path. These shortcuts never work, and the guilt we feel for having chosen them only compounds our feelings of despair. What is a pilgrim to do? Listen in on the whispers of Pilgrim and his companion, Hopeful, in their dungeon:

> Pilgrim: Brother, what shall we do? The life we now live is miserable. For my part I know not whether it is best to live, or to die.

> Hopeful: My brother, remember how valiant thou hast been heretofore? Apollyon could not crush thee, nor could all that thou didst hear, or see, or feel, in the Valley of the Shadow of Death. What hardship, terror and amazement hast thou already gone through. . . . remember how thou playedst the man at Vanity Fair, and was neither afraid of the chain, nor cage, nor yet of bloody death? . . .

> Now a little before it was day, good Christian, as one half amazed, broke out in this passionate speech: What a fool am I, to lie in a stinking dungeon when I may as well walk with liberty. I have a key in my bosom called Promise, that will open any lock in Doubting Castle.

Pilgrim lay in despair because he had forgotten. Hopeful urges him to *remember*, both all he had been through as well as the assurances he has from the One who called him on the journey. Life on the road requires recollection of our Love's past deeds on our behalf and his promise of continued faithfulness to us. We will need courage and patience and those are strengthened by remembering. We will need memory, which is to say, we will need *faith*.

Faith looks back and draws courage; hope looks ahead and keeps desire alive. And meantime? In the meantime we need one more item for our journey. To appreciate what it may be, we have to step back and ask, what is all this for? The resurrection of our heart, the discovery of our role in the Larger Story, entering into the Sacred Romance—why do we pursue these things? If we say we seek all of this for our own sake, we're right back where we started: lost in our own story. Jesus said that when a person lives merely to preserve his life, he eventually loses it altogether. Rather, he said, give your life away and discover life as it was always meant to be. "Self-help is no help at all. Self-sacrifice is the way, my way, to finding yourself, your true self" (Matt. 16:25, *The Message*). Self-preservation, the theme of every small story, is so deeply wrong because it violates the Trinity, whose members live to bring glory *to the others*. The road we travel will take us into the battle to restore beauty in all things, chief among them the hearts of those we know. We grow in glory so that we might assist others in doing so; we give our glory to increase theirs. In order to fulfill the purpose of our journey, we will need a passion to increase glory; we will need *love*.

Memory, imagination, and a passion for glory—these we must keep close at hand if we are to see the journey to its end. Dragons and nits and the noonday demons lie in wait. But the road is not entirely rough. There are oases along the way. It would be a dreadful mistake to assume that our Beloved is only waiting for us at the end of the road. Our communion with him sustains us along our path.

11

Desert Communion: Learning to Live on Heaven's Shores

> *Our nature makes us wish for rest, that is to say, an increase in being.*
>
> St. Augustine

WE'VE BEEN FOLLOWING the story line of the Sacred Romance for ten chapters since I (Brent) first posed the question in Chapter 1, "What is it that I am supposed to *do* as a Christian for the rest of my life?" Hopefully that question begins to dim for you as it does for me as the story line of the Sacred Romance begins to grip us. It is awesome to think that we are truly God's Beloved, the Bride he is preparing to reveal in all her beauty before the courts of heaven. It is joyous to consider that in his exotic goodness, he is even using the dragons and nits to free us into our true identities as sons and daughters of God, and collectively as the bride of Christ. We are indeed his Betrothed and have already received the first seal of his love in his Spirit that dwells in us.

Every courtship, at least every healthy one, is moving toward a deeper heart intimacy that is the ground for the consummation of the relationship spiritually, emotionally, and physically. The first question in the orthodox confessions of faith tests our awareness of this wonderful truth when it asks, "What is the chief end and purpose of man?" And the answer: "To know God and enjoy knowing him forever."

If we hear that answer as creatures of the Enlightenment, that is to say, the Age of Reason, the answer does not take our breath away. The word *know* has been captured in service of the intellect and so when we think of knowing God, images of learning more about him immediately come to mind. With a sigh, we consider what book we might buy or what Bible study we might attend to understand more clearly God's attributes. But what if we were sitting in a sidewalk café overhearing the following exchange between a fiancée and her betrothed?

She: "I'm so looking forward to our wedding day. I do love you so much. I really wish I could see more of you. There's so much about you I want to know better."

He: "Yes, dear, I know. I'm going to send you a book that describes more about my life. I'm sure you'll get a lot out of it."

She: "I'll be glad to read it. But I just want to hold your hand. [She continues somewhat mischievously.] I just want to kiss you."

He: "I'm sure you do, beloved. Let me send you a tape describing the role of physical affection at different stages of courtship. You'll find it worthwhile, I'm sure."

She: (Somewhat disappointed) "That's wonderful, darling. It's just that I so look forward to our wedding day. I want to be with you so badly. I think of us being, you know, 'together,' day and night."

He: "Yes, intimacy is important. I'd like to send you to a weekend seminar that really should be quite helpful."

About this time, most of us would say, "What a stiff. This guy doesn't have a clue how to love this woman. Why doesn't she dump him for somebody who's still breathing?" Yet, this is very much the way we often carry on our love affair with God. We picture him as being much like the man in the café, and so we sigh, try to push down our disappointment, and go on being good Christians. But listen with me to excerpts from another conversation between two lovers:

Lover: "How beautiful you are, my darling! Oh, how beautiful! Your eyes are doves."

Beloved: "How handsome you are, my lover! Oh, how charming! And our bed is verdant."

Lover: "Show me your face, let me hear your voice; for your voice is sweet, and your face is lovely. . . . Your mouth is like the best wine."

Beloved: "May the wine go straight to my lover, flowing gently over lips and teeth. I belong to my lover, and [your] desire is for me. Come, my lover, let us go to the countryside, let us spend the night in the villages. . . ."

Is this not a conversation that truly does begin to take our breath away? Do we not find ourselves wanting to follow these lovers to the country just to be close to such passion? This is not a conversation from the latest dime-store romance but from the Song of Solomon. God does not give us this look through the bedroom window at the love affair between Solomon and the Queen of Sheba just to be voyeuristic. As we turn from the window and look into his eyes, we realize that this is the kind of passion he feels for us and desires from us in return—an intimacy much more sensuous, much more exotic than sex itself.

Many of us would run to meet God in such a way if we only knew where to find him. But where . . . how is he to be found with this kind of intimacy? And, too, we don't go from being strangers to lovers in an instant. There are the conversations between a father and son or daughter to be held first, and the platonic intimacy of good friends. Some of us have had our hearts seared by the tainted desire of those who should have loved us platonically but rather used our desire for love to violate us emotionally and sexually. Our hearts shrink back from such imagery, as they will until we have received healing. Yet, the intimacy represented by married love is what God desires with each of us and so the imagery of courtship is what we must consider.

When we first think of being in a relationship with God, we probably picture him as somewhat flashy, even as many of us tried to be (at least us guys) when we were dating. He gave Jacob visions of angels descending and ascending to heaven; he parted the Red Sea for Moses and made the sun stand still for a day so the Israelites could win a battle. He definitely makes an impression. But you kind of wonder what he's like when you're alone with him. Would he just stay the life of the party, still playing to the crowd?

Two images from the Scriptures show us a very different side of God. In Revelation 2:17, John tells us that when we get to heaven, God will give us a white stone with a name on it that only he knows; the kind of name one lover calls another in private because it reveals something very personal about their relationship. A second picture of the way God desires to commune with us is found in 1 Kings 19 where we find the prophet Elijah worn out and afraid, fleeing from Jezebel. She has been trying to kill him ever since he did the same to her prophets. God tenderly ministers to Elijah, twice bringing him food and water. Elijah, strengthened, travels forty days and forty nights until he reaches Mt. Horeb, where he goes to sleep in a cave. The Lord wakes him and listens to his lament about what it is like to be God's prophet. Elijah is worn out from "doing" and badly in need of restoration of spirit. A great wind strikes the mountain, followed by an earthquake and a fire. And God is in none of these. Finally, Elijah hears a "gentle whisper." And it is in the gentle whisper that he finds God.

And so it is with us. God is not "out there somewhere" in some dramatic way, waiting to commune with us by earthquake or fire or signs in the sky. Instead, he desires to talk with us in the quietness of our own heart through his Spirit, who is in us.

It is his voice that has whispered to us about a Sacred Romance. What do you hear when you listen for that gentle, quiet voice?

What I so often hear, or feel, is a restlessness, a distractedness where it seems that dozens if not hundreds of disconnected or scattered thoughts vie for my attention. Bits and pieces of my smaller story, and sometimes major edifices, flash onto the screen: what other people think of me and what I need to do to win them. Anger, ego, lust, and simply blankness of spirit all take turns occupying my heart.

Indeed, when I first listen to my heart, what I often hear is the language and clatter of my old "lovers" and not much else. There seems to be no stillness or rest. If I try to hold still, my soul reacts like a feather in the afternoon breeze, flitting from place to place without purpose or direction. I almost seem invisible in the noise or blankness. Theologians refer to this condition as "ontological lightness," the reality that when I stop "doing" and simply listen to my heart, I am not anchored to anything substantive. I become aware that my very identity is synonymous with activity.

Many of us sense that this is true in our vocation, our religion, and even our recreation. When we are trying to get to know who people are, we typically ask what they do. I am a counselor. You are a businessman. It is how we tend to think of ourselves. In the religious arena, the question may take the form of what we believe. Ann Jones believes in consubstantiation, so she is a Lutheran. You believe in five-point Calvinism, so you are a Presbyterian. John Smith believes in fellowship suppers and informal worship services, so he is an evangelical.

Our whole American culture is infected with ontological lightness, celebrities and pro athletes being the most dramatic examples of this victimization of our souls that ruins us for any substantive love relationship. They are anchored only to their performances and out of their performances come their identities—and ours who worship them. As soon as they stop performing, their identities—and ours—disappear.

As men, if we have not anesthetized ourselves and become invisible by choice, we try to anchor ourselves to some form of competence. David Letterman, in a recent interview, basically said that his sense of himself was only grounded in the twenty-four-hour period between shows. If the last show was good, he felt good about himself. If the audience didn't respond, he felt horrible. Women in our culture, feminism notwithstanding, often try to ground themselves in being valued for their external beauty. Marilyn Monroe went to nightclubs disguised in a black wig long after she was famous to see if she could still attract a man as Norma Jean. She felt the emptiness as soon as she was no longer being flirted with, even after clearly establishing her identity as the world's most beautiful woman. And the emptiness consumed her in the end.

As Christians, we often feel the ungrounded restlessness of our ontological lightness even in our prayers. We find ourselves praying for God to "do" this, or for him to help us "do" that. Our prayers seem to originate from somewhere near the surface of our skin rather than any deep place inside. We go away feeling that we have not communed, that we have not put down our burdens, and indeed, we haven't.

Sinning is also a way of anchoring ourselves in a small romance that will give us a moment's satisfaction without losing control of the Arrows. Often when we are talking about a person who has lived a sinful life, we say what a "shell" she has become, ruefully pointing out that she has lost what once made her substantively human. C. S. Lewis, once again, captures the final condition of those who have never found themselves in his novel *The Great Divorce*. When the busload of citizens from hell go to the outskirts of heaven and step out of the bus, heaven's grass is so substantive that it hurts their feet to walk on it. They have become shadowy wraiths who are forced to expend tremendous amounts of energy just to take a step across heaven's meadows. Most of them return to the bus, preferring the "comfort" of hell.

We, too, experience the spiritual life not as a love affair, but as burdensome, heavy, exhausting and alien in our condition of ontological lightness. Jesus calls to us as his loved ones and says: "Come to me, all you who are weary and burdened, and I will give you rest. Take my yoke upon you and learn from me, for I am gentle and humble in heart, and you will find rest for your souls. For my yoke is easy and my burden is light" (Matt. 11:28–30).

And I find myself answering, "I don't know how to rest in you, Jesus. When I try to reach out for you, all I see are the outstretched arms of my old lovers waving, demanding, and enticing me back to them. All I can hear is the clatter of their voices. Where are you in all of this confusion?"

Two years ago, worn out by three years of spiritual battle, I found myself asking the question this way: "Jesus, if your Spirit abides in me in the person of the Holy Spirit, who is my Comforter, why do I so often feel alone and you seem so far away?" What came to me in response were Jesus' words in John 15:5, "I am the vine; you are the branches. If a man remains in me and I in him, he will bear much fruit; apart from me you can do nothing." Jesus was saying, "Living spiritually requires something more than just not sinning or doing good works. In order to live in the kingdom of heaven, you must abide in me. Your identity is in me."

If I'm not abiding in Jesus, then where is it that I abide? I asked myself.

I began to notice that when I was tired or anxious, there were certain sentences I would say in my head that led me to a very familiar place. The journey to this place would often start with me walking around disturbed, feeling as if there was something deep inside that I needed to put into words but couldn't quite capture. I felt the "something" as an anxiety, a loneliness, and a need for connection with someone. If no connection came, I would start to say things like "Life really stinks. Why is it always so hard? It's never going to change." If no one noticed that I was struggling and asked me what was wrong, I found my sentences shifting again to a more cynical level: "Who cares? Life is really a joke." Surprisingly, I noticed by the time I was saying those last sentences, I was feeling better. The anxiety was greatly diminished.

My "comforter," my abiding place, was cynicism and rebellion. From this abiding place, I would feel free to use some soul cocaine—a violence video with maybe a little sexual titillation thrown in, perhaps having a little more alcohol with a meal than I might normally drink—things that would allow me to feel better for just a little while. I had always thought of these things as just bad habits. I began to see that they were much more; they were spiritual abiding places that were my comforters and friends in a very spiritual way; literally, other lovers.

The final light went on one evening when I read John 15 in *The Message*. Peterson translates Jesus' words on abiding this way: "If you make yourselves at home with me and my words are at home in you, you can be sure that whatever you ask will be listened to and acted upon." Jesus was saying in answer to my question, "I have made my home in you, Brent. But you still have other comforters you go to. You must learn to make your home in me." I realized that my identity had something to do with simply "staying at home."

It also dawned on me that holiness, surprisingly, also comes not out of doing but out of staying at home, with who and where we are and with who and where God is in us. Indeed, we will only have the courage to leave home and continue to live as pilgrims out on the road if we have some sense that our true home abides within us in the Spirit of Christ and that we can do the same with him. And in the meantime, out of this abiding,

Jesus transforms us. Our identity begins to coalesce, not out of doing, but out of living with a good friend for a number of years and simply finding we have become more like him.

I began to see that there was a different heart journey that I had to take to learn to abide in Christ. It is the journey George MacDonald describes in his poem that I quoted in Chapter 9:

Tis hard for (us) to rouse (our) spirits up—
It is the human creative agony
Though but to hold the heart an empty cup
Or tighten on the team the rigid rein
Many will rather lie among the slain
Than creep through narrow ways the light to gain—
Than wake the will, and be born bitterly.
(*Diary of an Old Soul*)

By going to my abiding place of cynicism and rebellion, I was filling my heart cup with something that made the emptiness go away for a moment. I was "lying among the slain" rather than creeping out onto the unknown narrow path that leads to abiding in the comfort of Jesus. I began to reject the cynical thoughts when they came to comfort me and replace them with words of faith: "Jesus, I don't know how to heal myself of this anxiety. I don't even clearly understand it. But I will not anesthetize it with other lovers. I cling to you and trust in your healing."

At times, I experienced a different kind of peace. At other times, Jesus would bring certain of his words to mind: "I know the plans I have for you," he says in Jeremiah 29:11, "plans to prosper you and not to harm you, plans to give you hope and a future." Rather than indulge in my less-wild lovers, I began at times to tighten on the team the rigid rein and simply stand (rest) in faith. Spiritual warfare began to intensify as the adversary saw me not agreeing with him that life was hopeless and thus threatening to take away his footholds (perhaps strongholds) in my heart.

Besides these false comforters that we abide in, there are also the less-wild lovers I spoke of in Chapter 9 that are intertwined with our heart because they give us an identity. Whether it be accumulating great wealth, being seen as profound due to our knowledge and cleverness of speech, being physically attractive, or any of the hundreds of other small stories we have learned to abide in, we live in fear that we will sooner or later be exposed and our identities will be stripped from us. We redouble our efforts at "doing" to prevent this calamity, and again, in our ontological lightness, our lack of being anchored in anything substantive, we experience the spiritual life as burdensome and exhausting. We are unable to walk the meadows of the spiritual life.

We all want to be someone's hero or someone's beauty, to be in a relationship of heroic proportions. Contrary to legalistic forms of self-denial, we need to feel free to admit this without embarrassment. It is a core longing God himself placed within us and a deep part of our identity as men and women. It is in how we go about being heroes and beauties that is the issue. For each of us, the enemy has convinced us that we need our less-wild lovers and smaller stories to have an identity, indeed to even survive. Once we start depending on them for life, he sabotages our smaller stories so that we are exposed in our ontological lightness. Then he mocks us for our foolishness. He literally runs us into the ground with envy, anxiety, shame, discouragement, renewed efforts to rewrite our small stories so they work, and finally, depression and despair. Many of us are spiritually and emotionally ill from the process I've just described. What theo-logians have called "ontological lightness," Freud referred to as "hysteria." We are more familiar with it being called "neurosis." Jesus simply calls it the symptoms of our adultery.

"Come to me, all you who are weary and burdened, and *I* will give you rest," says Jesus. Most of us think of spiritual progress as requiring us to do more, even as our heart cries out to us to lay our burdens down. We renew our efforts at Bible study, Scripture memory, and Christian service, fearing that we will be discovered in our weakness and need. We try to use whatever small story we have been living in—competence, gifted speaking, service to others, and so on—to cross the chasm between living in the flesh and living spiritually, when only Christ can carry us to rest. The kinds of "doing" we have learned are not weighty enough to allow us to walk in the spiritual fields of the kingdom of God.

God speaks to Israel through the prophet Isaiah when she is surrounded by enemies and making every effort to appease them through diplomacy, gifts, treaties, and bribes, and says this to her:

> "You went to Molech with olive oil
> and increased your perfumes.
> You sent your ambassadors far away;
> you descended to the grave itself!
> You were wearied by all your ways,
> but you would not say, 'It is hopeless.'
> You found renewal of your strength,
> and so you did not faint" (Isa. 57:9–10).

God calls Israel to repent by admitting her weariness and fainting. Instead, she looks for ways to use her personal assets to redeem herself. Jesus spoke to the people about rest and thirst. The Pharisees demanded that they obey a constantly growing weight of religious laws and traditions, and chastised them for staggering under the load. They led people in the exact opposite direction from where their salvation lay—in admitting their weariness and fainting. As long as they hoped in their self-sufficiency, they would not call out to God and receive forgiveness, healing, and restoration.

So many of our contemporary churches operate on this same system of guilt. When our people are crying out for communion and rest, we ask them to teach another Sunday school class. When they falter under the load, we admonish them with Scriptures on serving others. One wonders what would happen if all activity motivated by this type of guilt were to cease for six months. Much of organized Christianity would collapse even as the Pharisees saw happen to their own religious system. As Jesus talked about thirst and rest, he brought people to the reality of their own heart.

It is impossible to live the spiritual life in the ontological lightness of doing because our hearts and minds become enemies rather than allies. Neither are we free to love or serve. The problem is not that people are not important enough to us. It is that they are *too* important—we need their approval too much in our ontologically light condition of living in our smaller stories.

God desires to use even the dragons and nits to reveal our true identities in all of our ontological density. God comes to the Israelites in Exodus 23:29–30 and tells them that he will not drive their enemies from the land in a day because they are not substantive enough to hold the land and it would become desolate and overrun with wild animals. He tells them that he will drive out their enemies as they become able to hold it. They must learn to rest in him. It is from the place of abiding in him that they will be able to hold on to what is theirs. James tells us in the introductory thoughts to his letter that we should count it all joy when we fall into various trials because God will use them to make us substantive. He tells us that this will happen as we learn to trust totally in God rather than halfway counting on our own devices with God as a fallback (being double-minded).

When we hear the phrase "trust totally in God," most of us probably sigh, hearing it as one more requirement that we have never been able to live up to. But what if we were to listen to our hearts, and hear it as a need to faint, a need to lay down our "doings" and simply make our needs known to Christ, and rest in him?

The Desert Tradition

How do we go about actually "doing" rest?

When Jesus was preparing for his public ministry, as well as his battle with Satan, he went to the desert—away from the synagogue, away from people, away from family and friends. Matthew tells us that God's Spirit led Jesus into the desert to be tempted by the devil. He prepared for spiritual battle by separating himself from all dependency on the provisions of this world, starting with the most basic: food. He fasted for forty days. He abided in prayer, in communion with his Father in heaven. When Satan came to test him with the things of this world, he answered him not with intellectual argument, but rested in the truth of Scripture. And when he had resisted the devil by abiding in the Spirit, angels came and ministered to him.

There is a place on each of our spiritual journeys where the Spirit also desires to lead us into the desert. We hear him calling to us in the restlessness and weariness of our own heart. The first time the Spirit speaks to us, we don't know it is him. We assume we are just not doing enough to be spiritual, and so we renew our religious efforts instead of fainting. Sometimes, like Samuel when God spoke to him in the night, we go through this process two or three times before we realize it is God speaking to us in our heart and follow him into the desert.

The desert tradition begun by Jesus was continued in the third and fourth centuries by a group of men and women known as "the Desert Fathers." They lived in caves and simple dwellings in the deserts south of Israel and committed themselves to prayer, solitude, and silence along with a separation from the provisions of this world. "Society," says Thomas Merton in *The Wisdom of the Desert*, "was regarded [by the Desert Fathers] as a shipwreck from which each single individual had to swim for his life. . . . These were men who believed that to let oneself drift along, passively accepting the tenets and values of

what they knew as society, was purely and simply a disaster."
Adds Henri Nouwen, in *The Way of the Heart*, "Without solitude, we remain acolytes of our society and continue to be
entangled in the illusions of the false self."

In order to learn who we really are, we must have a place in
our lives where we are removed from the materialism, entertainment, diversion, and busyness that the Vanity Fair of our
society and culture immerse us in. The things sold at the booths
in the Fair are tranquilizers that separate us, and protect us,
from the emptiness and need of our heart. As we leave these
less-wild lovers behind and enter into solitude and silence in our
own desert place, the first thing we encounter is not rest, but
fear, and a compulsion to return to activity. In *The Ascent to
Truth*, Thomas Merton says,

> We look for rest and if we find it, it becomes intolerable. Inca-
> pable of the divine activity which alone can satisfy [rest] . . . fallen
> man flings himself upon exterior things, not so much for their
> own sake as for the sake of agitation which keeps his spirit pleas-
> antly numb . . . [The distraction] diverts us aside from the one
> thing that can help us to begin our ascent to truth . . . the sense of
> our own emptiness.

"In the middle of the road of my life," says Dante, "I awoke
in a dark wood." Our emptiness is often the first thing we find
when we face honestly the story going on in our heart. It is the
desert's gift to us. George MacDonald encourages us to
embrace it as a friend by "leaving the heart an empty cup," and
proceeding. But what do we do with our emptiness if we stay
with our heart? If we try to pray, our minds fill with busy, disconnected petitions that start with the words, "God, help me to
do this or that better, have more faith, read the Bible more."
The busy petitions of our minds seem to leave something inside
our chest cavity unexpressed, something that is trying to tell us
about the way things are.

"Our mind is busy with oughts," says Nouwen in *The Way*

of the Heart, while "the heart instructs us on what is. The renewing of our mind takes place through our hearts." He quotes Theophan, the recluse, who says, "To pray is to descend with the mind into the heart, and there to stand before the face of the Lord, ever present, all-seeing, within you." If we allow our mind simply to listen, we perhaps begin to hear our heart speak—faintly, beneath the clatter. It says, "I am so weary, so lost. I have no energy to redeem myself. How I long for rest."

Our mind hears these words and realizes it is of no use to ask God to give us energy to make our way back up the cliff over which we have fallen. We need the Good Shepherd to come and get us. If we allow our heart to give our mind the words to pray, we say, "Jesus, help me. All my lovers have failed me. Forgive me. I cannot quench my thirst. Give me the water of life."

Not long ago, I was preparing one of my lectures for the Sacred Romance series that John and I were presenting in Colorado Springs. John's talk the week before had deeply touched people with the understanding of God's grace and love for them. A friend came by the table where I was sitting in our neighborhood bagel shop and kiddingly remarked, "My husband says his life was changed after last week's talk, so you better come up with something good."

Part of my smaller story has been to use my gifts as a teacher and thinker to win people's admiration—to be someone's hero. At the thought that perhaps I might be the second-best speaker in this series, I was overcome with waves of shame, a feeling of being exposed. The adversary was quickly there with reminders of past failures and the resulting pain. For a minute, I considered redoubling my efforts to come up with a good talk that week—to look up new quotes, find a really good movie clip to illustrate my points.

But this particular time, I simply listened to what my heart was telling me. It spoke to me about weariness and the fear of being found lacking; of having nothing that would make me anyone's hero. I left the bagel shop and drove to the open space that surrounds our neighborhood. I got out and began walking, feeling deeply agitated and dejected over being trapped in such a foolish place. Anyone who has ever had the thing you depended on for life threatened will know what I am describing. I had no energy to think up prayers or even any sense of what to pray for. I began to repeat a simple sentence in my head, "Jesus, you are faithful to cleanse me from all my sins." I did not try to exegete it or convince myself to believe it. I simply let it linger and resonate between my head and heart for whatever Jesus chose to do with it. After not many minutes, I felt something begin to break up deep down inside, a feeling of loneliness and longing acknowledged. There was a release that brought tears. I sensed that Jesus was ministering to me in a quiet and tender way, in a place years distant and much deeper in my spirit than just feelings provoked by the events of that particular morning. A sensation of freedom and well-being rose up from the very place inside that moments ago had felt such agitation.

Bringing what was happening back up into my head in order to put words to it, I can only say it was as if Jesus were telling me, "I understand your ache, Brent. I know how you've wanted to be someone's hero. It's okay. Rest in my love." There were no words of admonishment or exhortations to try harder. I understood, in some ways for the first time, that my sin really *has* been cleansed by Jesus and is no longer an issue between us. I knew in my heart, in a way I perhaps hadn't before, the depth of Jesus' love for me on the cross. I felt like I was home.

Resting in Jesus is not applying a spiritual formula to ourselves as a kind of fix-it. It is the essence of repentance. It is letting our heart tell us where we are in our own story so that Jesus can minister to us out of the Story of his love for us. When, in a given moment, we lay down our false self and the smaller story of whatever performance has sustained us, when we give up everything else but him, we experience the freedom of knowing that he simply loves us where we are. We begin just to *be*, having our identity anchored in him. We begin to experience our spiritual life as the "easy yoke and light burden" Jesus tells us is his experience. We become ontologically substantive.

In Matthew 24, Jesus tells us that in the last days, people will have lost the Sacred Romance altogether. Having no anchor, their faith will grow cold and they will be literally swept away in panic, as all but what cannot be shaken, is shaken. Only those of us who are securely anchored in him in our heart will be left standing to share the Sacred Romance with those who are lost.

We have come to the shores of heaven together, to the border of the region where our Christianity begins to move from a focus on doing to one of communion with Christ, our Lover and Lord. The spiritual disciplines of silence, solitude, meditation (heart prayer), fasting, and simplicity practiced by Christ and passed on to us by the traditions of the Desert Fathers bring us through our emptiness and thirst into the presence of God. Many fine books have been written on the practice of the spiritual disciplines, among them, *Celebration of the Disciplines and Prayer*, by Richard Foster; *The Way of the Heart*, by Henri Nouwen; and *The Spirit of the Disciplines*, by Dallas Willard. I recommend these as resources to help the reader journey more deeply into God's heart, which is our true home.

When we begin to abide in God's heart, the blades of grass on heaven's outskirts no longer puncture our feet. Here and there, a fresh and exotic scent reaches us from heaven's very borders. From my own experience of it, I liken it to a trip my family and I took to the Grand Canyon five years ago. Finally, after hours on end of traveling through the dry, featureless terrain of Arizona's deserts, we began climbing through the pine forests of the Kaibab Plateau, heading toward the Grand Canyon. The higher we drove, the clearer the air seemed to become, and the sweeter the scent of pine. We wondered aloud that we had been so uncomfortable hours before. The canyon itself came on us in a lavender and pink and yellow hugeness that swept my breath away. Even though I knew it was coming and that we would soon see it, I was not prepared for its exotic, spiritual beauty. I wept in joy without really understanding why. And I knew there were many days of beauty and exploration ahead.

Such will be the coming kingdom of heaven.

12

Coming Home

*The door on which we have been knocking all our lives
will open at last.*

C. S. Lewis

MY WIFE, Stasi, reads the end of novels first. Until recently, I (John) never understood why. "I want to know how the story ends, to see if it's worth reading," she explained. "A story is only as good as its ending. Even the best stories leave you empty if the last chapter is disappointing.

"But the opposite is also true," she added. "A really tragic story can be saved by a happy ending."

"But doesn't knowing the end take away the drama?" I asked.

"It only takes away the fear and frees you to enjoy the drama. Besides, some things are too important to be left to chance," she said, and turned back to her book.

A story is only as good as its ending. Without a happy ending that draws us on in eager anticipation, our journey becomes a nightmare of endless struggle. Is this all there is? Is this as good as it gets? On a recent flight I was chatting with one of the attendants about her spiritual beliefs. A follower of a New Age guru, she said with all earnestness, "I don't believe in heaven. I believe life is a never-ending cycle of birth and death." *What a horror*, I thought to myself. *This Story had better have a happy ending*. St. Paul felt the same. If this is as good as it gets, he said, you may as well stop at a bar on the way home and tie one on; go to Nordstrom's and max out all your credit cards; bake a cake and eat the whole thing. "Let us eat and drink, for tomorrow we die" (1 Cor. 15:32).

Our hearts cannot live without hope. Gabriel Marcel says that "hope is for the soul what breathing is for the living organism." In the trinity of Christian graces—faith, hope, and love—love may be the greatest but hope plays the deciding role. The apostle Paul tells us that faith and love depend on hope, our anticipation of what lies ahead: "Faith and love . . . spring from the hope that is stored up for you in heaven" (Col. 1:5). Our courage for the journey so often falters because we've lost our hope of heaven—the consummation of our Love Story. No wonder we live like Robinson Crusoe, trying to cobble together the best life we can from the wreckage of the world; we think we're stuck here forever. Of course, our less-wild lovers seem irresistible—we see them as our only shot at some relief. The reason most men, to quote Thoreau, "live lives of quiet desperation" is that they live without hope.

Several years ago I joined some friends for a weekend of fly-fishing on the Snake River in Jackson Hole, Wyoming. It was a last fling of fall, before the long winter set in with my heavy responsibilities at home, work, and in grad school. I had looked forward to the adventure for months, but the weekend hadn't lived up to my expectations. The weather was lousy, the fishing dreadful. As the weekend drew to a close, I found myself tense and irritable, trying desperately to squeeze joy out of diminishing hopes. *This is it?* I thought to myself. *This is as good as it's going to be?* Standing together in the river Saturday evening, empty-handed, my friend announced almost as an afterthought that he had arranged a float down a wild section of the river with a famous guide for our last day together. The weather was predicted to be clear and the fishing was practically guaranteed to be fabulous.

In a moment, everything changed. The evening light took on a rich, golden quality; the fall colors became vivid; I noticed the musical rushing of the waters for the first time and my fishing buddies suddenly seemed to me a truly decent bunch of guys. The pressure I had placed on the vacation was lifted as my heart recovered hope. I was released by the promise of better things to come.

The story may seem silly (particularly for those who do not fly-fish), but it reveals one of the most important truths of the human heart: If for all practical purposes we believe that this life is our best shot at happiness, if this is as good as it gets, we will live as desperate, demanding, and eventually despairing men and women. We will place on this world a burden it was never intended to bear. We will try to find a way to sneak back into the Garden and when that fails, as it always does, our heart fails as well. If truth be told, most of us live as though this life *is* our only hope, and then we feel guilty for wanting to do exactly what Paul said he would do if that were true.

In his wonderful book *The Eclipse of Heaven*, A. J. Conyers put it quite simply: "We live in a world no longer under heaven." All the crises of the human soul flow from there. All our addictions and depressions, the rage that simmers just beneath the surface of our Christian facade, and the deadness that characterizes so much of our lives has a common root: We think this is as good as it gets. Take away the hope of arrival and our journey becomes the Battan death march. The best human life is unspeakably sad. Even if we manage to escape some of the bigger tragedies (and few of us do), life rarely matches our expectations. When we do get a taste of what we really long for, it never lasts. Every vacation eventually comes to an end. Friends move away. Our careers don't quite pan out. Sadly, we feel guilty about our disappointment, as though we ought to be more grateful.

Of course we're disappointed—we're made for so much more. "He has also set eternity in the hearts," (Eccl. 3:11). Our longing for heaven whispers to us in our disappointments and screams through our agony. "If I find in myself desires which nothing in this world can satisfy," C. S. Lewis wrote, "the only logical explanation is that I was made for another world."

If faith and love hang on hope, if a life without hope is as Paul says "to be pitied" (1 Cor. 15:19), then shouldn't we devote ourselves to recovering a vision for the end of our story in as vivid colors as our imagination can conceive?

I knew a man who as a young boy hated the idea of heaven. He would puzzle and embarrass his Sunday school teachers by stating quite boldly, whenever the subject of heaven was brought up, that he didn't want to go there. Finally, one of them had the sense to ask him why. His answer? "I don't like peas." He had heard the familiar Christmas carol "Silent Night," with the lovely refrain "Sleep in heavenly peace" and thought it referred to the vegetable. Like any red-blooded boy he figured there had to be better things to do.

Our images aren't much better. We speak so seldom of heaven and when we do, the images are sickly: fat babies fluttering around with tiny wings, bored saints lazing on shapeless clouds, strumming harps and wondering what's happening back on earth where the real action is.

The crisis of hope that afflicts the church today is a crisis of *imagination*. Catholic philosopher Peter Kreeft writes:

> Medieval imagery (which is almost totally biblical imagery) of light, jewels, stars, candles, trumpets, and angels no longer fits our ranch-style, supermarket world. Pathetic modern substitutes of fluffy clouds, sexless cherubs, harps and metal halos (not halos of *light*) presided over by a stuffy divine Chairman of the Bored are a joke, not a glory. Even more modern, more up-to-date substitutes—

Heaven as a comfortable feeling of peace and kindness, sweetness and light, and God as a vague grandfatherly benevolence, a senile philanthropist—are even more insipid. Our pictures of Heaven simply do not move us; they are not moving pictures. It is this aesthetic failure rather than intellectual or moral failures in our pictures of Heaven and of God that threatens faith most potently today. Our pictures of Heaven are dull, platitudinous and syrupy; therefore, so is our faith, our hope, and our love of Heaven. . . . It doesn't matter whether it's a dull lie or a dull truth. Dullness, not doubt, is the strongest enemy of faith, just as indifference, not hate, is the strongest enemy of love. (*Everything You Wanted to Know About Heaven*)

If our pictures of heaven are to move us, they must be moving pictures. So go ahead—dream a little. Use your imagination. Picture the best possible ending to your story you can. If that isn't heaven, something better is. When Paul says, "No eye has seen, no ear has heard, no mind has conceived what God has prepared for those who love him" (1 Cor. 2:9), he simply means we cannot outdream God. What is at the end of our personal journeys? Something beyond our wildest imagination. But if we explore the secrets of our heart in the light of the promises of Scripture, we can discover clues. As we have said from Chapter 1, there is in the heart of every man, woman, and child an inconsolable longing for intimacy, for beauty, and for adventure. What will heaven offer to our heart of hearts?

Intimacy

Our longing for intimacy gives us the greatest scent of the joys that lie ahead. Being left out is one of life's most painful experiences. I remember the daily fourth-grade torture of waiting in line while the captains chose their teams for the kickball games. As each captain took turns choosing a player, descending from best to worst, our rank in fourth-grade society was reinforced. Though others fared worse than I—"Don't make us take

Smitty, we had him last time"—I was never the first to be chosen. No one ever said, "Wait—we get Eldredge this time!" I didn't feel wanted; at best, I felt tolerated. And then there was junior high cafeteria. After buying lunch, you carried your tray out into the dining room, looking for a place to eat. There was an unspoken hierarchy that determined where you could sit. One day, I dared to test that caste system. With modest courage I walked over to the table filled with the "cool" kids, but before I could sit down, one of them sneered, "Not here, Eldredge, we're saving this for someone else."

These are some of the ways I learned the lesson that I was on the outside. Throughout our lives, each one of us lives with a constant nagging that we never quite fit in, we never truly belong. We've all had enough experiences to teach us that we will never be allowed into the "sacred circle," the place of intimacy. Even those who are chosen to be part of the "in" crowd are never chosen for who they truly are. So we hide parts of ourselves to try and fit in, or kill our desire to be an insider, rather than let our longing lead us toward the true intimacy for which we were designed.

On the other hand, there is the joy of having someone save a place for us. We walk into a crowded room at church or at a dinner party and someone across the way waves us over, pointing to a chair he's held on to especially for us. For a moment we feel a sense of relief, a taste of being on the inside. Now consider Jesus' words in John 14:2—"I am going . . . to prepare a place for you." Christ promises that he is saving a place in heaven especially for each of us. When we walk into the crowded excitement of the wedding feast of the Lamb, with the sound of a thousand conversations, laughter and music, the clinking of glasses, and one more time our heart leaps with the hope that we might be let into the sacred circle, we will not be disappointed. We'll be welcomed to the table by our Lover himself. No one will have to scramble to find another chair, to make room for us at the end of the table, or rustle up a place setting. There will be a seat with our name on it, held open at Jesus' command for us and no other.

Heaven is the beginning of an adventure in intimacy, "a world of love," as Jonathan Edwards wrote, "where God is the fountain." The Holy Spirit, through the human authors of Scripture, chose the imagery of a wedding feast for a reason. It's not just any kind of party; it is a *wedding* feast. What sets this special feast apart from all others is the unique intimacy of the wedding night. The Spirit uses the most secret and tender experience on earth—the union of husband and wife—to convey the depth of intimacy that we will partake with our Lord in heaven. He is the Bridegroom and the church is his bride. In the consummation of love, we shall know him and be known. There we shall receive our new name, known only to our Lover, which he shall give to us on a white stone (Rev. 2:17).

George MacDonald, a theologian with a poet's heart, has explored the promises of heaven more richly than perhaps any other man. He explains what the stone implies:

> It is the man's own symbol—his soul's picture, in a word—the sign which belongs to him and to no one else. Who can give a man this, his own name? God alone. For no one but God sees what the man is. . . . It is only when the man has become his name that God gives him the stone with the name upon it, for then first can he understand what his name signifies. . . . Such a name cannot be given until the man *is* the name . . . that being whom He had in His thought when He began to make the child, and whom He kept in His thought through the long process of creation that went to realize the idea. To tell the name is to seal the success—to say "In thee also I am well pleased." (*Unspoken Sermons*)

The stone will free us to enjoy the riches of heaven, for in order to share in this heavenly intimacy, we must have the freedom of heart enjoyed by Adam and Eve before the Fall, who were naked and *felt no shame*. This is the freedom from sin, or as Kreeft has said, "from what makes us not ourselves. We will be free to be the true selves God designed us to be." Shame kills intimacy. The soul that still is in some way hiding cannot enjoy the fullness of knowing what characterizes the love between God and the saints in heaven. But then we shall be perfect; our loved ones will be perfect as well. All that has ever stood between us will be swept away and our heart will be released to real loving. The intimacy that begins between God and his people will be enriched and echoed by our communion with each other. The deepest longing of our heart—our longing to be part of the sacred circle, to be inside—reveals to us the greatest of the treasures heaven has in store. For we were made in and for the most sacred circle of all. Lewis says,

> The sense that in this universe we are treated as strangers, the longing to be acknowledged, to meet with some response, to bridge some chasm that yawns between us and reality, is part of our inconsolable secret. And surely, from this point of view, the promise of glory, in the sense described, becomes highly relevant to our deep desire. For glory meant good report with God, acceptance by God, response, acknowledgment, and welcome into the heart of things. The door on which we have been knocking all our lives will open at last. (*The Weight of Glory*)

Beauty

"And they all lived happily ever after." Where? Doing what? As wonderful as it will be to have our longing for relationship filled to overflowing, it is not enough. Our heart has other longings that heaven draws forth. There is so much more to the human soul and so much more to the riches God has prepared for those who love him. In the same way that life sharpens our yearning to be welcomed into the sacred circle of intimacy, so it awakens another ache from deep within—our longing for beauty.

The Ritz Carlton Laguna Beach is one of the most luxurious hotels in southern California. Nestled on a bluff above its private cove with white sandy beach, the hotel exudes romance. Its mediterranean architecture lifts the Ritz out of space and time, creating a fairy-tale ambiance. Arches and tile walkways lead to fountained courtyards and terraces with breathtaking views of the Pacific. The tropical climate nourishes a lush canopy of purple and red bougainvillea, whimsical flower gardens, rich green lawns, and swaying palms. Staying at the Ritz, one can almost forget, if for a moment, that the Fall ever happened. Stasi and I enjoyed a weekend of escape there thanks to a business conference I was asked to attend.

Late one evening I slipped away from the meeting to wander the grounds alone. I felt restless inside and thought a walk might be calming. Something drew me through the terraces toward the ocean. As I wandered over the beautifully manicured lawns, more luxuriant than any carpet, the sounds of music and laughter from parties inside mingled with the scent of the flower beds in the warm ocean breeze. My restlessness grew. Standing on the edge of the cliff with the crashing of the waves below and the shining of the stars above, I felt the restlessness swell into an ache. As Simone Weil said, there are only two things that pierce the human heart: beauty and affliction. I was run clean-through by the beauty of it all, overcome by an ache for a home I have never seen.

I have had this experience many times, whether walking along the Napali Coast in Hawaii, flying over the glaciers of Alaska, or noticing the simple rays of sunshine falling on the kitchen table. Yet it always takes me by surprise. We grow so used to living in a world soiled by the Fall that our soul's desire for beauty lies dormant deep within, waiting for something to awaken it. During a visit to Westminster Cathedral in England, a friend of mine got lost and by accident came into that glorious sanctuary by a rather commonplace side door. Stepping around the corner he was totally unprepared for the majesty he suddenly found himself engulfed by: the sweeping architecture, the glory in stone and spire and glass. At that very moment a choir broke into song, their angelic harmonies filling the massive cathedral. "I don't know what happened," he later told me, "but I broke down and began to weep."

"Each and every instance of beauty," writes Mark Helprin, "is a promise and example, in miniature, of life that can end in balance, with symmetry, purpose and hope." We long for beauty and the promise that it speaks. Our revulsion to the ugly is the counterpart to our desire for beauty. I used to hate the part of my daily commute that took me through the worst sections of Washington, D.C.: abandoned buildings, burned-out cars, desolate neighborhoods. It was a symbol of the triumph of evil, chaos, and death. My heart grieved to see such devastation and I breathed a sigh of relief as I passed through the wreckage and drove into the farmlands of Maryland. But we must be careful here; as Lewis said, one of the mistakes we so often make when captured by an object of beauty, whether it's a place, a person, or a work of art, is to assume the longing in our heart is for the thing before us. The Ritz and Westminster and farm meadows—these are shadows of the realities to come. The beauty of the tabernacle carried by Israel through the desert was a type of the real item in heaven. So it goes with all things on earth: The beauty that so captures our heart and is so fleeting draws us toward the eternal reality.

We long for beauty, and when the biblical writers speak of heaven, they use the most beautiful imagery they can. You can almost hear the agony of the writer trying to get it right while knowing he falls far short of what he sees. In the book of Revelation, St. John uses the word *like* again and again. "And He who was sitting was like a jasper stone and a sardius in appearance; and there was a rainbow around the throne, like an emerald in appearance. . . . Before the throne there was . . . a sea of glass like crystal" (4:3, 6 NASB). The beauty cannot be captured, only alluded to by the most beautiful things on earth.

I believe the beauty of heaven is why the Bible says we shall be "feasted." It's not merely that there will be no suffering, though that will be tremendous joy in itself; to have every Arrow we've ever known pulled out and every wound dressed with the leaves from the tree of life (Rev. 22:2). But there is more. We will have glorified bodies with which to partake of all the beauty of heaven. As Edwards wrote, "Every faculty will be an inlet of delight." We will eat freely the fruit of the tree of life and drink deeply from the river of life that flows through the city. And the food will satisfy not just our body but our soul. As Lewis said,

> We do not want merely to *see* beauty, though, God knows, even that is bounty enough. We want something else which can hardly be put into words—to be united with the beauty we see, to pass into it, to receive it into ourselves, to bathe in it, to become part of it. (*The Weight of Glory*)

And so we shall.

Adventure

What will we do in heaven? The Sunday comics picture saints lying about on clouds, strumming harps. It hardly takes your breath away. The fact that most Christians have a gut sense that earth is more exciting than heaven points to the deceptive powers of the enemy and our own failure of imagination. What do we do with the idea of "eternal rest"? That sounds like the slogan of a middle-class cemetery. We know heaven begins with a party, but then what? A long nap after the feast? The typical evangelical response—"We will worship God"—doesn't help either. The answer is certainly biblical, and perhaps my reaction is merely a reflection on me, but it sounds so one-dimensional. Something in my heart says, *That's all? How many hymns and choruses can we sing?*

We will worship God in heaven, meaning all of life will

finally be worship, not round after round of "Amazing Grace." The parable of the minas in Luke 19 and the talents in Matthew 25 foreshadow a day when we shall exercise our real place in God's economy, the role we have been preparing for on earth. He who has been faithful in the small things will be given even greater adventures in heaven. We long for adventure, to be caught up in something larger than ourselves, a drama of heroic proportions. This isn't just a need for continual excitement, it's part of our design. Few of us ever sense that our talents are being used to their fullest; our creative abilities are rarely given wings in this life. When Revelation 3 speaks of us being "pillars in the temple of our God," it doesn't mean architecture. Rather, Christ promises that we shall be actively fulfilling our total design in the adventures of the new kingdom.

Act IV—heaven—is the continuation of the Story that was interrupted by the Fall. God made the earth and entrusted it to us, to bring order and increase beauty. We were to be his regents, reigning with his blessing and authority. That arrangement was corrupted by the Fall so that the earth no longer responds to our leadership as it once did. When Christ accomplished our redemption, he didn't do it to place us on the bench for eternity. He restored us to put us back in the game. He even subjected the earth to a time of futility until the day it will be "liberated from its bondage to decay and brought into the glorious freedom of the children of God" (Rom. 8:21). We will then co-reign with Christ. "St. Peter for a few seconds walked on the water," Lewis reminds us, "and the day will come when there will be a re-made universe, infinitely obedient to the will of glorified and obedient men, when we can do all things, when we shall be those gods that we are described as being in Scripture."

Part of the adventure will be to explore the wonders of the new heaven and new earth, the most breathtaking of which will be God himself. We will have all eternity to explore the mysteries of God, and not just explore, but celebrate and share with one another. Here is a remarkable thing to consider: Your soul has a unique shape that fits God. We are not all the same, but unique creations each of us. Therefore, as MacDonald says,

> Every one of us is something that the other is not, and therefore knows something—it may be without knowing that he knows it—which no one else knows: and . . . it is everyone's business, as one of the kingdom of light and inheritor in it all, to give his portion to the rest. (*Unspoken Sermons*)

This may be why the angels Isaiah sees flying around the throne room of God are crying "holy, holy, holy," not to God, but "*to one another*" (6:3, italics mine). They are calling each other to see what they see of the majesty and beauty of God, so that their joy might be increased as they celebrate Him together. Every experience of delight takes on a fuller dimension when we share it. This is why we so often feel in the midst of some wonderful moment, "how I wish my beloved were here."

The exploration of heaven shall also include our knowing of each other. How could it not? How can love be complete without the freedom to be naked and unashamed? More than unashamed, we shall be *celebrated*. It is one of the sorrows of our present life: the separation we feel even from those closest to us. Married people can be the loneliest on earth, not for some failure of the marriage, but because they have tasted the best there is of human relationships and know it is not all it was meant to be. In *A Tale of Two Cities*, Charles Dickens captures that sense of mystery each human soul is to another.

> A wonderful fact to reflect upon, that every human creature is constituted to be that profound secret and mystery to every other. A solemn consideration, when I enter a great city by night, that every one of those darkly clustered houses encloses its own secret; that every room in every one of them encloses its own secret; that every beating heart in the hundreds of thousands of breasts there, is, in some of its imaginings, a secret to the heart nearest it!

But in heaven that veil shall be removed as well, not to our shame and embarrassment, but to our utter delight. Remember, we will be perfect, meaning we will be the soul that God had in mind all along. And then, as MacDonald says,

> We shall have the universe for our own, and be good merry children in the great house of our father. I think then we shall be able to pass into and through each other's very souls as we please, knowing each other's thought and being, along with our own, and so being *like* God. When we are all just as loving and unselfish as Jesus; when, like him, our one thought of delight is that God is, and is what he is; when the fact that a being is just another person from ourselves is enough to make that being precious. (*The Heart of George MacDonald*)

And there is, of course, the exploration of our own lives. We know a time will come for us to look back with our Lord over the story of our lives. Every hidden thing shall be made known, every word spoken in secret shall be uttered. My soul shrinks back; how will this not be an utter horror? The whole idea of judgment has been terribly twisted by our enemy. One evangelistic tract conveys the popular idea that at some point shortly upon our arrival in heaven the lights will dim and God will give the signal for the videotape of our entire life to be played before the watching universe: every shameful act, every wicked thought. How can this be so? If there is "*now* no condemnation for those who are in Christ Jesus" (Rom. 8:1, *italics mine*), how is it possible there will be shame later? God himself shall clothe us in white garments (Rev. 3:5). Will our Lover then strip his beloved so that the universe may gawk at her? Never.

However God may choose to evaluate our lives, whatever memory of our past we shall have in heaven, we know this: It will only contribute to our joy. We will read our story by the light of redemption and see how God has used both the good and the bad, the sorrow and the gladness for our welfare and his glory. With the assurance of total forgiveness we will be free to know ourselves fully, walking again through the seasons of life to linger over the cherished moments and stand in awe at God's grace for the moments we have tried so hard to forget. Our gratitude and awe will swell into worship of a Lover so strong and kind as to make us fully his own.

Arrival

Brent and I have tried to put words to many of the questions we believe every heart is asking. Well into the Christian journey, two new questions began to haunt us: Will I make it to the end? and, Will it be good when I get there?

Several years into our marriage Stasi and I reached one of the lowest moments of our lives. Sitting over the breakfast table one morning, the subject of divorce was raised in a rather casual way, as if it were a question about the raspberry jam. We had drifted apart, I knew that, but until that moment I didn't realize just how far. Over the next few days I made an emergency plan. We would go to the mountains for a holiday in hopes of recovering some of the ground we had lost. We had honeymooned in Yosemite and I thought that might be the place to look again for a lost romance.

We set out the day after Christmas on a warm and sunny morning. But as the hours wore on, a snowstorm was building in the mountains ahead. Evening fell and with it came the snow, softly at first, then heavier and harder. Our car began to slip and spin on the icy road. It was dark when we reached the entrance to the park. Up ahead, I could see the cars before us turning around and heading back down the mountain. *Oh Lord,* I prayed, *please—not now, not when so much is riding on this.* The ranger told us that the roads had become treacherous and a blizzard was raging higher in the mountains. Several cars had already slid off the highway. He recommended we turn back but left the choice to us.

"We're going on," I said. As the hours dragged on, the snow blanketed the road and dark woods all around. We were alone. *Will we make it?* I wondered to myself. *Can it possibly be good even if we do?* My knuckles were white from clutching the steering wheel. The tension in the car was thick, a palpable reminder of the reason we had come.

Just when I was about to abandon hope, twinkling lights appeared through the trees ahead. As we rounded the bend, the Wawona Hotel came into view—a gorgeous, white Victorian inn with garlands hanging from the balcony and a massive Christmas tree in the window. The snowfall eased and the flakes were now falling softly, gently. We could see a fire roaring in the large stone fireplace, casting a romantic glow over the couples who lingered over dinner. Currier and Ives never printed a more beautiful scene. As I pulled our car into safety, a deer ambled from the woods and across the white meadow before us. The sense of arrival was almost too much to bear. We had made it! The beauty of it all seemed to speak the promise of a life restored. As we walked into our room, we discovered a bottle of champagne on ice—a gift some friends had sent ahead. That weekend we turned a corner in our marriage and began the healing we now enjoy.

For now, our life is a journey of high stakes and frequent danger. But we have turned the corner; the long years in exile are winding down and we are approaching home. There is no longer any question as to whether we will make it and if it will be good when we get there. "I am going there to prepare a place for you," Jesus promised. "And if I go and prepare a place for you, I will come back and take you to be with me" (John 14:2–3).

One day soon we will round a bend in the road and our dreams will come true. We really will live happily ever after. The long years in exile will be swept away in the joyful tears of our arrival home. Every day when we rise, we can tell ourselves, *My journey today will bring me closer to home; it may be just around the bend.* All we long for we shall have; all we long to be, we will be. All that has hurt us so deeply—the dragons and nits, the Arrows and our false lovers, and Satan himself—they will all be swept away.

And then real life begins.

EPILOGUE
Remembering Toward Heaven

The Road goes ever on and on
Down from the door where it began.
Now far ahead the Road has gone,
And I must follow, if I can,
Pursuing it with eager feet,
Until it joins some larger way.
                                        J. R. R. Tolkien

THE SACRED ROMANCE calls to us every moment of our lives. It whispers to us on the wind, invites us through the laughter of good friends, reaches out to us through the touch of someone we love. We've heard it in our favorite music, sensed it at the birth of our first child, been drawn to it while watching the shimmer of a sunset on the ocean. It is even present in times of great personal suffering—the illness of a child, the loss of a marriage, the death of a friend. Something calls to us through experiences like these and rouses an inconsolable longing deep within our heart, wakening in us a yearning for intimacy, beauty, and adventure. This longing is the most powerful part of any human personality. It fuels our search for meaning, for wholeness, for a sense of being truly alive. However we may describe this deep desire, it is the most important thing about us, our heart of hearts, the passion of our life. And the voice that calls to us in this place is none other than the voice of God.

We set out to discover if there is in the wide world out there a reality that corresponds to the world within our heart. Hopefully, we have helped you see in new ways that Chesterton was right: Romance *is* the deepest thing in life; it is deeper even than reality. Our heart is made for a great drama, because it is a reflection of the Author of that story, the grand Heart behind all things. We've seen how we lose heart when we lose the eternal Romance, which reminds us that God sought to bring us into his sacred circle from all eternity, and that despite our rejection of him, he pursues us still. The Arrows and the Haunting both find their place in Act III of that drama, in which we now live. But this act is drawing to a close. Our Lover has come to rescue us in the person of Jesus; he has set our heart free to follow him up and into the celebration that begins the adventures of Act IV.

Where do we go from here? "This life," wrote Jonathan Edwards, "ought to be spent by us only as a journey towards heaven." That's the only story worth living in now. The road goes out before us and our destination awaits. In the imagery of Hebrews, a race is set before us and we must run for all we're worth. Our prayers will have been answered if we've helped to lift some of the deadweight so that your heart may rise to the call, hear it more clearly, respond with "eager feet." Our final thoughts echo the advice found in Hebrews 12:2–3:

> Let us fix our eyes on Jesus, the author and perfecter of our faith, who for the joy set before him endured the cross, scorning its shame, and sat down at the right hand of the throne of God. Consider him who endured such opposition from sinful men, so that you will not grow weary and lose heart.

This marvelous passage is familiar to many of us, so lest we should become dull to its power due to its familiarity, consider Eugene Peterson's translation from *The Message*:

> Keep your eyes on *Jesus*, who both began and finished this race we're in. Study how he did it. Because he never lost sight of where he was headed—that exhilarating finish in and with God—he could

put up with anything along the way: cross, shame, whatever. And now he's *there*, in the place of honor, right alongside God. When you find yourselves flagging in your faith, go over that story again, item by item, that long litany of hostility he plowed through. *That* will shoot adrenaline into your souls!

Jesus remembered where he was headed and he wanted to get there with all his heart. These two themes, memory and desire, will make all the difference in our journey ahead. Without them, we will not run well, if we run at all. We have tried to do honor to the riches of memory and desire in the preceding chapters of this book. Let me (John) explore them more deeply now, as a man goes through his essential belongings one last time before setting out on a long and dangerous quest.

Living from Desire

Jesus ran because he wanted to, not simply because he had to or because the Father told him to. He ran "for the joy set before him," which means he ran out of *desire*. To use the familiar phrase, his heart was fully in it. We call the final week of our Savior's life his Passion Week. Look at the depth of his desire, the fire in his soul. Consumed with passion, he clears the temple of the charlatans who have turned his Father's house into a swap meet (Matt. 21:12). Later, he stands looking over the city that was to be his bride but now lies in the bondage of her adulteries and the oppression of her taskmasters. "O Jerusalem, Jerusalem," he cries, ". . . how often I have *longed* to gather your children together, as a hen gathers her chicks under her wings, but you were not willing" (Matt. 23:37, *italics mine*). As the final hours of his greatest struggle approach, his passion intensifies. He gathers with his closest friends like a condemned criminal sitting down to his last meal. He alone knows what is about to unfold. "I have *eagerly desired* to eat this Passover with you," he says, "before I suffer" (Luke 22:15, italics mine). Then on he presses, through the intensity of Gethsemane and the passion of the cross. Is it possible he went through any of it halfheartedly?

When the going gets rough, we're going nowhere without desire. And the going will get rough. The world, the minions of darkness, and your own double-mindedness are all set against you. Just try coming alive, try living from your heart for the Sacred Romance and watch how the world responds. They will hate you for it and will do everything in their power to get you to fall back into the comfort of the way things were. Your passion will disrupt them, because it sides with their own heart which they've tried so hard to put away. If they can't convince you to live from the safer places they have chosen, they will try intimidation. If that fails, they'll try to kill you—if not literally, then at the level of your soul.

Jeremiah lived the struggle of desire. He knew the deep ambivalence of living for the Sacred Romance. His decision to trust in the love of God and join the battle for the hearts of his people made him an outcast, a pariah. Like the Master he served, he was "despised and rejected by men." After years of opposition, getting tossed naked into the bottom of wells, plots against his life, the shame of false accusations and the loneliness of isolation, Jeremiah has had it. He is ready to throw in the towel. He lets the passion of his soul forth, directly at God:

> O LORD, you deceived me, and I was deceived;
> you overpowered me and prevailed.
> I am ridiculed all day long;
> everyone mocks me. . . .
> So the word of the LORD has brought me
> insult and reproach all day long.
> But if I say, "I will not mention him
> or speak any more in his name,"
> his word is in my heart like a fire,
> a fire shut up in my bones.
> I am weary of holding it in;
> indeed, I cannot. *(20:7–9)*

This aching prophet gives words to the dilemma of desire. He says, in effect, "You put this Romance in my heart, you drew me out on this wild adventure—how could I keep from following? But now that I have, it has only brought me the fury of my community. And what's worse, I cannot walk away. I'm trapped by my desire for you." Jeremiah may have become a prophet initially out of a sense of duty, but now he is caught up in the Sacred Romance because he can't help it. Paul voiced the same dilemma: "Woe to me if I do not preach the gospel!" (1 Cor. 9:16). When the going gets rough, *ought* is not enough to keep you going.

You may recall the movie *Chariots of Fire*, which tells the story of two Olympic runners: Eric Liddell and Charles Abrams. Both are passionate about running, but in very different ways. Abrams runs because he is driven; he runs in order to prove something. He is a cheerless man whose whole life is motivated by ought, by duty, by the law. Liddell runs because he can't help it. "When I run," he says, "I feel God's pleasure." He knows a freedom of heart that Abrams can only watch from a distance. Abrams uses discipline to subdue and kill his heart. Liddell is so freed by grace that when he runs, Abrams says, "He runs like a wild animal—he unnerves me." "Where," Liddell asks, "does the power come from to see the race to its end? It comes from *within*." It comes from desire.

"The whole life of the good Christian," said Augustine, "is a holy longing." Sadly, many of us have been led to feel that somehow we ought to want less, not more. We have this sense that we should atone for our longings, apologize that we feel such deep desire. Shouldn't we be more content? Perhaps, but contentment is never wanting *less*; that's the easy way out. Anybody can look holy if she's killed her heart; the real test is to have your heart burning within you and have the patience to enjoy what there is now to enjoy, while waiting with eager anticipation for the feast to come. In Paul's words, we "groan inwardly as we wait eagerly" (Rom. 8:23). Contentment can only happen as we increase desire, let it run itself out toward its fulfillment, and carry us along with it. And so George Herbert prayed,

> Immortal Heat, O let thy greater flame
> Attract the lesser to it: let those fires,
> Which shall consume the world, first make it tame;
> And kindle in our hearts such true desires,
> As may consume our lusts, and make thee way.
> Then shall our hearts pant thee. (*Love*)

There may be times when all we have to go on is a sense of duty. But in the end, if that is all we have, we will never make it. Our Hero is the example. He's run on before us and he's made it, he's there now. His life assures us it can be done, but only through passionate desire *for the joy set before us*. Or, as Peterson has it, "that exhilarating finish in and with God." The road ahead will take us into a deepening and a focusing of our desire. As author James Houston has experienced, "The desire that really gives life is to know God. This desire is never satisfied, for it is one that grows with its fulfillment; and our relationship with God changes and leads to a constant deepening of our desires" (*The Heart's Desire*).

As our soul grows in the love of God and journeys forth toward him, our heart's capacities also grow and expand: "Thou shalt enlarge my heart" (Ps. 119:32 KJV). A friend of mine is a missionary to Muslims in Senegal. He tells me that after conversion, Muslims will often notice flowers for the first time. Prior to salvation, Muslims in that arid country live a very utilitarian existence. Things are valued only for what they can do. Their houses are dull and drab; trees are only appreciated if they are fruit trees; if they have a function. It is as if the Muslims have lived without beauty for their whole lives and now, having their souls released from bondage, they are freed into the pleasures of God's creative heart. I'm struck by the parallels to modern fundamentalism. Their hatred of pleasure is not a sign of their godliness; quite the opposite. The redeemed heart hungers for beauty.

But the sword cuts both ways. While our heart grows in its capacity for pleasure, it grows in its capacity to know pain. The two go hand in hand. What, then, shall we do with disappointment? We can be our own enemy, depending on how we handle the heartache that comes with desire. To want is to suffer; the word *passion* means to suffer. This is why many Christians are reluctant to listen to their hearts: They know that their dullness is keeping them from feeling the pain of life. Many of us have chosen simply not to want so much; it's safer that way. It's also godless. That's stoicism, not Christianity. Sanctification is an awakening, the rousing of our souls from the dead sleep of sin into the fullness of their capacity for life.

Desire often feels like an enemy, because it wakes longings that cannot be fulfilled in the moment. In the words of T. S. Eliot,

> "April is the cruelest month, breeding
> Lilacs out of the dead land, mixing
> Memory and desire" (*The Waste Land*).

Spring awakens a desire for the summer that is not yet. Awakened souls are often disappointed, but our disappointment can lead us onward, actually increasing our desire and lifting it toward its true passion.

I am a lucky man. I have a family and friends who love me well. But they also let me down. When I feel the pain of their failure, I have several options. I can retreat into cynicism ("Isn't that the way life really is?") and deaden the pain by killing my desire. Or I can become more demanding ("You will never do that again"), manipulating them and in a way increasing my addiction to relationship. Or I can let it be a reminder that a day is coming when we will all live in perfect love. I can let the ache lead me deeper into my heart and higher toward heaven. And this is where memory comes in. Desire keeps us moving forward; memory keeps us moving in the right direction.

Rehearsing the Story

If we choose the way of desire, our greatest enemy on the road ahead is not the Arrows, nor Satan, nor our false lovers. The most crippling thing that besets the pilgrim heart is simply forgetfulness, or more accurately, the failure to remember. You *will* forget; this isn't the first book you've read in search of God. What do you remember from the others? If God has been so gracious as to touch you through our words, it will not have been the first time he has touched you. What have you done with all the other times? I have had enough encounters with God to provide a lifetime of conviction—why don't I live more faithfully? Because I forget.

I am humbled by the story of the golden calf. These people, the Jews God has just delivered from Egypt, have seen an eyeful. First came the plagues; then the Passover; then the escape from Pharaoh's armies and last-minute rescue straight through the Red Sea. After that came the manna: breakfast in bed, so to speak, every morning for months. They drank water from a rock. They heard and saw the fireworks at Mt. Sinai and shook in their sandals at the presence of God. I think it's safe to say that this band of ransomed slaves had reasons to believe. Then their leader, Moses, disappears for forty days into the "consuming fire" that enveloped the top of the mountain, which they could see with their own eyes. While he's up there, they blow the whole thing off for a wild bacchanalian party in honor of an idol made from their earrings. My first reaction is arrogant: How could they possibly be so stupid? How could they forget everything they've received straight from the hand of God? My second is a bit more honest: That's me; I could do that; I forget all the time.

Spiritual amnesia is so likely that from Genesis to Revelation, the Scriptures are full of the call to remember. "Only be careful," says our Lover, "and watch yourselves closely so that you do not forget the things your eyes have seen or let them slip from your heart as long as you live" (Deut. 4:9). How then can we keep these things in our hearts? How can we, in the words of Dan Allender, "reclaim the treasures of memory for our life's journey"? The author of Hebrews answers, "Rehearse the story. Go over it item by item—particularly the central scene."

The cross of Christ is, as T. S. Eliot said, "the stillpoint in a turning world." Everything before leads up to it; everything that follows flows from it. It is the climax of the story, the centerpiece of the whole drama. As Paul says, "For what I received I passed on to you as of first importance: that Christ died for our sins according to the Scriptures, that he was buried, that he was raised on the third day according to the Scriptures, and that he appeared to Peter, and then to the Twelve" (1 Cor. 15:3–5).

We must be careful here or these will only be religious words. We interpret them, they carry meanings and associations for us. And the true meaning gets lost if we forget either the Story of which this scene is the climax or its meaning for our own story. *How* we remember is as important as *what* we remember. It seems impossible that the truths about the death and resurrection of Jesus could become lost or rote, but it happens all the time. Witness the number of dead, lifeless churches in your own city. This is inevitable when we fail to remember, or when we remember only with a purely propositional approach to Scripture. We can possess volumes of doctrinal knowledge and it can all be true, but if it is separated from reality—especially the life of the heart—it becomes of no consequence to us. Robert Jenson uses this example:

At various places in the New Testament, Jesus' death is called a "sacrifice," in order to make its meaning instantly clear. In the ancient world, sacrifices were offered on every street corner, and every infant understood what they were supposed to accomplish. When Christian preachers said, "Jesus' death has done what sacrifices attempt to do," the light was turned on, and hearers could respond, "So that is what is supposed to be so great about him. . . ." Preachers still talk about Jesus as the "great sacrifice," but then have to spend twenty minutes explaining what that means. If the gospel thereby gets said at all—which is unlikely—it is the subsequent explanation that does it and not the propositions with "sacrifice." (*Story and Promise*)

This is why we must remember the death and resurrection of Jesus of Nazareth in the larger context of the Sacred Romance. That Story gives the propositions their significance.

On the other hand, the truth of the gospel becomes meaningless when all we have is "story." Was this Jesus divine, or merely a great man? The question fostered a major controversy for the church in the fourth century. Leaders on both sides of the debate started with the same narrative (the Gospels) but came to very different conclusions. The Council of Nicea was called, from which we get the Nicene Creed, one of the central articles of the church and a defining propositional statement on the divinity of Christ. Brent and I have taken a great risk in our use of the story motif, because in the twentieth century liberal theologians have used "narrative" as a way of dismantling any objective interpretation of Scripture. However, we cannot escape the fact that the Scriptures are given to us in the shape of a story.

Our acts of remembering must therefore involve both essential truths and dramatic narrative. I believe we need to hold the creeds in one hand and our favorite forms of art in the other. There are films, books, poems, songs, and paintings I return to again and again for some deep reason in my heart. Taking a closer look, I see that they all tell me about some part of the Sacred Romance. They help wake me to a deeper remembrance. As Don Hudson has said, "Art is, in the final analysis, a window on heaven."

Now that we are on our way, Satan will do everything he can

to steal the Romance. One way he does this is to leave us only propositions, or worse, "principles," like "the management techniques of Jesus" or "the marketing methods of Jesus." The heart cannot live on facts and principles alone; it speaks the language of story and we must rehearse the truths of our faith in a way that captures the heart and not just the mind.

Let us return again to that central scene and see what it is the author of Hebrews wants us to see in order to follow our Hero in the race ahead. How did Jesus sustain his passionate heart in the face of brutal opposition? *He never lost sight of where he was headed.* He had a vision for the future that was grounded in the past. In the story of the Last Supper, we are told that Jesus knew "he had come from God and was returning to God," and lived his life of selfless love to the end. He remembered both where he had come from and where he was going (John 13:3). And so must we.

Where We Have Come From

We rehearse the Sacred Romance because it interprets the rest of our experience. As Jenson says, "The story about Jesus is gospel because it is the key to our stories." Part of our journey forward is a journey backward into our stories, to bring all the events of our lives—the Arrows and the Haunting—into the light of the Sacred Romance for their proper interpretation. Answers mean nothing without real questions. We lost heart initially because we had no one to tell us how to reconcile the Haunting and the Arrows, or if we did, our interpreters often got the story wrong. Redemptive remembering is where we develop a life script by interpreting the past, with both the Arrows and the Haunting, in a way that gives energy to the present and direction to the future.

If we refuse to go and get them, the Arrows will remain lodged within us, poisoning the waters of our heart, coloring our real convictions about life and draining away our vitality for the journey. Several years ago a friend at work took me aside to say, "I don't know if you're aware of this, but you are intimidating your colleagues." I wanted to laugh, because I didn't feel intimidating at work; much of the time I felt small and scared. But his words provoked a search that led me first to the realization that I was in fact a very driven person (the reason my colleagues experienced me as intimidating). As I began to wonder why, I journeyed back to the day I was arrested as a teenager and the Arrow that lodged with the message "You are on your own." Though I had been a Christian for many years and knew all the promises about God always being with me, they had no power in my soul. The Arrow remained defining and I lived from its perspective.

As I entered into that heart-room where this particular Arrow had struck, the wound felt tender and new. With Brent's help, I was able to bring it into the light of the Sacred Romance for God to touch, heal, and reinterpret. Standing again in that place, I had ears to hear Jesus tell me I am not on my own, that he will never leave or forsake me. Faced with a real question, the real answer meant something. The healing process is still under way and there are days when I can be a driven man, but much less so than before. That Arrow has lost its power. But it would still be there if all I had done was tell myself, "Be nicer to the people at work."

Where We Are Headed

Redemptive remembering also reclaims the Haunting we've known. I want to own a ranch; it is one of my most frequent daydreams. Does that come as a surprise? My most romantic moments in life came as a boy on my grandfather's ranch and there is a part of me that so wants to return to those golden summer days. The pull is especially powerful when life is pressing in and really requiring me to be a man. Somewhere in my heart, I want to be a boy again, riding in Pop's pickup. The longing is good, but it can remain trapped in time, attached to a particular place. I just received a letter from my grandmother telling me she sold the ranch. What am I to do with that part of my heart? Is it sold off with the ranch; does it die with the passing of that era?

Sometimes, we need to lose the very things that have brought us a taste of the Romance in order for our heart to move toward the real thing. Otherwise they become a false transcendence. The most unredemptive kind of remembering is what many people call "nostalgia." How sad to visit elderly friends and relatives to find them sitting around listlessly, pining for "the good old days." They have no life in the present and little vision for the future, because they are locked in the past. So even our best memories can prevent our running the race set before us until we see them in the light of the real Romance. My last visit to the ranch was such a time. As I walked into the back porch, the sound of the screen door brought a flood of memories. I felt again in that moment how "called out" I felt by my grandfather in those days. And then it struck me that it was *God* calling me out through my grandfather, and he calls me still. The Sacred Romance honors those memories by revealing them for what they are: hints of a deeper reality. I yearn for the day when I shall be forever young, free to ride the fields of heaven with my grandfather, my father, and my sons.

Finally, we were meant to remember together, in community. We need to tell our stories to others and to hear their stories told. We need to help each other with the interpretation of the Larger Story and our own. Our regular times of coming together to worship are intended to be times of corporate remembrance. "This, God has done," we say; "this, He will do." How different Sunday mornings would be if they were marked by a rich retelling of the Sacred Romance in the context of real lives. This is a far cry from the fact-telling, principle listing, list keeping that characterizes much of modern worship.

One of the reasons modern evangelicalism feels so thin is because it is merely modern; there is no connection with the thousands of years of saints who have gone before. Our community of memory must include not only saints from down the street, but also those from down the ages. Let us hear the stories of John and Teresa from last week, but also those of St. John of the Cross and Teresa of Avila, to name only two. Let us draw from that "great cloud of witnesses" and learn from their journeys, so that our memory may span the story of God's relationship with his people.

Remembering is not mere nostalgia; it is an act of survival, our way of "watching over our hearts with all diligence." In *The Brothers Karamazov*, the gentle Alyosha says, "And even if only one good memory remains with us in our hearts, that alone may serve some day for our salvation." Jesus seems to capture this moment in the parable of the prodigal son. It's a classic story of how one man tries to capture the Romance through the false transcendence of wine, women, and song. His small story collapses in on him and it appears all is lost. There, in the pigsty, he is on the verge of destruction. Would it not have been easy enough for him to kill his heart with sentences like, "This is where it all ends. This is what life is truly about. Whatever it was my heart was searching for, it is all a lie. There is no real Romance and I am nothing but a fool." The drama of this parable is so true to life. He raises that last arrow, ready to drive it through his heart, when suddenly, he *remembers*. And he hits the road for home.

When I consider all that is at stake in this journey I am on, how vulnerable are my heart and the hearts of those I love, how quickly I forget, I am moved to fall on my face and cry out to God for the grace to remember. George MacDonald says it better in poetry.

Were there but some deep, holy spell, whereby
Always I should remember thee. . . .
Lord, see thou to it, take thou remembrance's load:
Only when I bethink me can I cry;
Remember thou, and prick me with love's goad.
When I can no more stir my soul to move,
And life is but the ashes of a fire;
When I can but remember that my heart
Once used to live and love, long and aspire—
Oh, be thou then the first, the one thou art;
Be thou the calling, before all answering love,
And in me wake hope, fear, boundless desire.
            (*Diary of an Old Soul*)

The final burden of remembrance does not rest on us; if it did, we should all despair. Returning to the passage from Hebrews that I quoted earlier, Jesus is called the "author and perfecter of our faith" (12:2). He is the One who put the romance in our hearts and the One who first opened our eyes to see that our deepest desire is fulfilled in him. He started us on the journey and he has bound himself to see us through. Even though we may for long seasons forget him, he does not forget us.

"I am always with you;
you hold me by my right hand
You guide me with your counsel,
and afterward you will take me into glory. . . .
My flesh and my heart may fail,
but God is the strength of my heart
and my portion forever" (*Ps. 73:23, 26*).

Nor will he leave us without reminders along the way. "The world is fairly studded and strewn," writes Annie Dillard, "with unwrapped gifts and free surprises . . . cast broadside from a generous hand." Our heart can be restored to life and the smallest things become heavy with transcendence when we ask one simple question: What is this telling me about the Sacred Romance?

This summer, I found it in the crickets. After tucking my boys in bed, with the requisite several glasses of water, trips to the potty, and prayers, the house finally grew quiet. I stood at the upstairs window looking out on our backyard and in the darkness, with the warm breeze caressing my face, I listened. Perhaps it was the long winter then behind us, perhaps it was the long winter of the soul that went along with it, but there was in the song of the crickets something that released my heart. Memories of all the summers past rose and mingled with the promise of the summer that would now come again. Beneath that, something deeper spoke, something at once young and yet very old. It whispered the promise of the summer that was soon coming, which would never pass into fall.

Bibliography

Buechner, Frederick. *Son of Laughter*. San Francisco: Harper San Francisco, 1993.

———. *Telling Secrets*. San Francisco: Harper San Francisco, 1991.

———. *Telling the Truth: The Gospel as Tragedy, Comedy and Fairy Tale*. San Francisco: Harper and Row, 1977.

Dickens, Charles. *A Tale of Two Cities*. New York: Portland, 1988.

Dillard, Annie. *Teaching a Stone to Talk*. New York: Harper and Row, 1982.

Donne, John. *Donne*. New York: Knopf, 1995.

Dooley, David, ed. *The Collected Works of G. K. Chesterton*. Vol. I. San Francisco: Ignatius, 1986.

Frost, Robert. *Robert Frost's Poems*. New York: Washington Square Press, 1946.

Groom, Winston. *Forrest Gump*. Produced by Steve Tisch and Wendy Fineman; directed by Robert Zemekis. Paramount Pictures, 1994.

Hein, Rolland, ed. *The Heart of George MacDonald*. Wheaton: Harold Shaw, 1994.

Hutchinson, F. E., ed. *The Works of George Herbert*. Oxford: Oxford University Press, 1972.

Houston, James. *The Heart's Desire*. Oxford: Lion, 1992.

Jenson, Robert. *Story and Promise*. Ramsey: Siglar, 1989.

Kierkegaard, Sooren. *Philosophical Fragments.*, trans. David Swenson. Princeton, NJ: Princeton University Press, 1962. As quoted in Yancey, Philip. *Disappointment with God*. New York: Harper Paperbacks, 1988.

Kreeft, Peter. *Everything You Ever Wanted to Know About Heaven But Never Dreamed of Asking*. San Francisco: Ignatius, 1990.

Lewis, C. S. *The Great Divorce*. New York: Simon and Schuster, 1946; Touchstone, 1996.

———. *The Lion, the Witch, and the Wardrobe*. New York: Macmillan, 1950; Collier Books, 1970.

———. *Perelandra*. New York: Macmillan, 1944.

———. *The Weight of Glory*. Grand Rapids: Eerdmans, 1949.

MacDonald, George. *Diary of an Old Soul*. Minneapolis: Augsburg, 1994.

———. *Unspoken Sermons*. As Quoted in Lewis, C. S., ed. *George MacDonald: 365 Readings*. New York: Macmillan, 1947.

Maclean, Norman. *A River Runs Through It*. Chicago: Univ. of Chicago Press, 1976.

May, Gerald. *Addiction and Grace*. San Francisco: Harper San Francisco, 1988.

McGrath, Alister. *A Passion for Truth*. Downers Grove, IL: InterVarsity, 1996.

Merton, Thomas. *The Ascent To Truth*. San Diego: Harcourt and Brace, 1951.

———. *The Wisdom of the Desert*. New York: New Directions, 1960, 1963. Quoted in Henri J. M. Nouwen, *The Way of the Heart*. New York: Ballantine Books, 1981.

Nouwen, Henri J. M. *The Way of the Heart*. New York: Ballantine Books, 1981.

Ricks, Christopher, ed. *Milton: Paradise Lost and Paradise Regained*. New York: Signet, 1968.

St. John of the Cross. *The Living Flame of Love.*, trans David Lewis. London: Thomas Baker, 1934.

Tugwell, Simon. *Prayer*. Ireland: Veritas.

Van Leeuwen, Mary Stewart. *Prism*, February 1995.

Wiersbe, Warren, ed. *The Annotated Pilgrim's Progress*. Chicago: Moody, 1980.

Wilcox, David. "Show the Way"; © 1994 Irving Music, Inc., and Midnight Ocean Bonfire Music (BMI). Used by permission of Warner Brothers Publications U.S., Inc., Miami, FL 33014.

Wright, William Aldis. *The Complete Works of William Shakespeare*. Garden City, NY: Garden City, 1936.

Yancey, Philip. *Disappointment with God*. New York: Harper Paperbacks, 1988.

About the Authors

The late **Brent Curtis** was a counselor in private practice and the author of the book *Guilt*, published in 1992 by NavPress. He was killed in a climbing accident in 1998.

John Eldredge is the founder and director of Ransomed Heart™ Ministries in Colorado Springs, Colorado, a fellowship devoted to helping people recover and live from their deep heart. John is the author of numerous books, including, *Waking the Dead, Wild at Heart, The Sacred Romance,* and *The Journey of Desire.* John lives in Colorado with his wife, Stasi, and their three sons, Samuel, Blaine, and Luke. He is an avid outdoorsman who loves being in the wild.

To learn more about John's seminars, audiotapes, and other resources for the heart, visit him on the Web at:

www.RansomedHeart.com

Or write:

Ransomed Heart™ Ministries
P.O. Box 51065
Colorado Springs, CO 80949-1065

An excerpt from *The Journey of Desire*
By John Eldredge

OUR HEART'S DEEPEST SECRET

We are never living, but hoping to live.

—Pascal

It seems to me we can never give up longing and wishing while we are alive. There are certain things we feel to be beautiful and good, and we must hunger for them.

—George Eliot

And I still haven't found what I'm looking for.

—U2

There is a secret set within each of our hearts. It often goes unnoticed, we rarely can put words to it, and yet it guides us throughout the days of our lives. This secret remains hidden for the most part in our deepest selves. It is the desire for life as it was meant to be. Isn't there a life you have been searching for all your days? You may not always be aware of your search, and there are times when you seem to have abandoned looking altogether. But again and again it returns to us, this yearning that cries out for the life we prize. It is elusive, to be sure. It seems to come and go at will. Seasons may pass until it surfaces again. And though it seems to taunt us, and may at times cause us great pain, we know when it returns that it is priceless. For if we could recover this desire, unearth it from beneath all other distractions, and embrace it as our deepest treasure, we would discover the secret of our existence.

You see, life comes to all of us as a mystery. We all share the same dilemma—we long for life and we're not sure where to find it. We wonder if we ever do find it, can we make it last? The longing for life within us seems incongruent with the life we find around us. What is available seems at times close to what we want, but never quite a fit. Our days come to us as a riddle, and the answers aren't handed out with our birth certificates. We must journey to find the life we prize. And the guide we have been given is the desire set deep within, the desire we often overlook or mistake for something else or even choose to ignore.

The greatest human tragedy is to give up the search. Nothing is of greater importance than the life of our deep heart. To lose heart is to lose everything. And if we are to bring our hearts along in our life's journey, we simply must not, we cannot, abandon this desire. Gerald May writes in *The Awakened Heart*,

> There is a desire within each of us, in the deep center of ourselves that we call our heart. We were born with it, it is never completely satisfied, and it never dies. We are often unaware of it, but it is always awake . . . Our true identity, our reason for being, is to be found in this desire.

The clue as to who we really are and why we are here comes to us through our heart's desire. But it comes in surprising ways, and often goes unnoticed or is misunderstood. Once in a while life comes together for us in a way that feels good and right and what we've been waiting for. These are the moments in our lives that we wish could go on forever. They aren't necessarily the "Kodak moments," weddings and births and great achievements. More often than not they come in subtler, unexpected ways, as if to sneak up on us.

Think of times in your life that made you wish for all the world that you had the power to make time stand still. Are they not moments of love, moments of joy? Simple moments of rest and quiet when all seems to be well. Something in your heart says, *Finally—it has come. This is what I was made for!*

WHISPERS OF JOY

It was the final evening of our summer vacation. We had spent nine wonderful days in the Tetons hiking and swimming, laughing and playing, enjoying rare and wonderful time together as a family in a stunningly beautiful place. During our explorations, we had discovered a quiet pond in the woods, about a half hour's walk from camp, where wildlife would often come in the evening. This night, we planned to arrive at dusk and stay until night fell to see what nature might reveal. The sun was setting behind us as we arrived, and far off in the east massive thunderheads were building above the Absarokas, cloud upon cloud, giant castles in the sky. The fading day was slowly turning them peach, then pink, then gray.

A pair of trumpeter swans were swimming across our little pond, looking for all the world like something from a fairy tale. My wife and I sat together with our three boys on a spot of grass near the water's edge, our backs against a fallen log. Across the pond lay a meadow, the stage for the evening's drama. As light began to fade, a bull moose with a massive rack emerged from the willows directly across the meadow from where we sat. He spotted us and stopped; we held our breath. Silently, he disappeared into the trees as mysteriously as he had come. Before we could be disappointed, a cow moose and her calf appeared from another part of the meadow, wandering along grazing. We watched them as night continued to fall.

A cool breeze stirred the pines above us. Crickets began their twilight chorus. The cow lay down in the tall grass, but we could still see her calf. Sandhill cranes were calling and answering one another around the marsh with their haunting, primeval cries. The boys huddled closer to us. A beaver swam by our feet, making a V through the surface of the pond, faded with the light to a gunmetal gray. Far off in the distance, lightning was beginning within those cloud fortresses, flashes of glory. A small herd of elk came out to graze at the far end of the meadow, just as darkness was settling in. Finally, as if not to be left out, a lone coyote began to howl. It was one of the most breathtaking nights I have ever experienced in the wilderness, a living work of art. As the Scottish poet George MacDonald knew so well, something is calling to us in moments like these.

> Yet hints come to me from the realm unknown;
> Airs drift across the twilight border land,
> Odored with life;
> . . . whispers to my heart are blown
> That fill me with a joy I cannot speak,
> Yea, from whose shadow words drop faint and weak.
>
> (*Diary of an Old Soul*)

I know these years are passing quickly, and the time will come when our boys will no longer want to vacation with us.

They will find other loves and form other ties, and our lives will never be the same again. Sitting there with them in the woods, clutching their flashlights, whispering to each other about each passing mystery, I would have given anything to stop the clock, turn it back if only for a few days, let us live it all again. But the seasons pass with or without our permission, and I knew in my heart we could not stay. For a moment, we were all caught up in something bigger and more beautiful than we had ever known, "suspended above the earth," as Norman MacLean says, "free from all its laws, like a work of art. And I knew just as surely and just as clearly, that life is not a work of art, and that the moment could not last."

ECHOES FROM THE PAST

Sometimes these moments go unrecognized as they unfold, but their secret comes to us years later in our longing to relive them. Aren't there times in your life that if you could, you would love to return to? I grew up in Los Angeles but spent my boyhood summers in Oregon where both my mother's and my father's parents lived. There was a beauty and innocence and excitement to those days. Woods to explore, rivers to fish, grandparents to fuss over me. My parents were young and in love, and the days were full of adventures I did not have to create or pay for, but only live in and enjoy. Rafting and swimming in the Rogue River. Playing in the park. Huckleberry pie at Becky's along the road to Crater Lake. We all have places in our past when life, if only for a moment, seemed to be coming together in the way we knew in our hearts it was always meant to be.

There was a time when meadow, grove, and stream,
The earth, and every common sight,

To me did seem
Appareled in celestial light,
The glory and the freshness of a dream . . .
Heaven lies about us in our infancy;
Shades of the prison-house begin to close
Upon the growing boy,
But he beholds the light, and whence it flows.
He sees it in his joy; . . .
At length the man perceives it die away,
And fade into the light of common day.
(*Ode, Intimations of Immortality from Recollection of Childhood*)

Wordsworth caught a glimpse of the secret in his childhood, saw in it hints from the realm unknown. We must learn the lesson of these moments, or we will not be able to bring our hearts along in our life's journey. For if these moments pass, never to be recovered again, then the life we prize is always fading from view, and our hearts with it. It isn't until the kids are out of the house that you realize how precious were those years. The inflatable pool in the backyard. The stockings hung up at Christmastime. First steps and first home runs and first dates. We fill photo albums with all these moments, trying to hang on to them somehow. We hate to see them slip away. Our losses seem to say that the life we prize will never be ours, never come to stay. But the secret is coming to us even in our greatest losses.

SHOUTS OF LAMENT

I did not know how much Brent meant to me until I lost him. He was killed last year at this time, in a climbing accident. We had taken a group of men to the mountains on a retreat, believing that to help a man recover his heart, you must take him out of the office, away from the television, and into the wild. We planned three days at a ranch in Colorado where we would bring rock climbing, fly fishing, and horse-back riding together with talks on the journey of a man's heart. Brent was leading the climbing on day two when he fell. The loss was unspeakable for many, many people. Ginny lost her husband. Ben and Drew lost their daddy. Many people lost the only man who had ever fought for their hearts.

I lost the truest friend I have ever known. Brent was more than my partner; he was for me the rarest of gifts—his heart saw what mine saw. Our friendship was a shared journey, a mutual quest, for the secret of our souls. It took us into the mountains, into literature and music, into the desperate battle raging all around for the hearts of others as well. We laughed and grieved and scorned and yearned all along the way. When he lost his son in a mountaineering accident, Nicholas Wolterstorff wrote,

> There's a hole in the world now . . . A center, like no other, of memory and hope and knowledge and affection which once inhabited this earth is gone. Only a gap remains. A per-spective in this world unique in this world which once moved about in this world has been rubbed out . . . There's nobody who saw just what he saw, knows what he knew, remembers what he remembered, loves what he loved . . . Questions I have can never now get answers. The world is emptier. (*Lament for a Son*)

This is silly, really, and a little embarrassing, but I find myself turning suddenly when I see a silver gray Jeep pass by. I look to see if it is his, if he is there. Brent is gone; I know that. How I know that. But still, I find myself doing a double take when I see a Jeep like his. Something rises in me, something beyond reason. A hope that perhaps it is his, that he is driving past me again. The other day I was in a parking lot and saw a beat-up old Cherokee with a rack on top. I stopped, went over, and looked. I know in my head that this is ridiculous. Brent is gone. But my heart refuses at some level to accept it. Or rather, my yearning for things to be right is so strong that it overrides my logic and turns my head, in hope against hope, every time.

"The heart," Blaise Pascal said, "has its reasons which reason knows not of." Something in us longs, hopes, maybe even at times believes that this is not the way things were supposed to be. Our desire fights the assault of death upon life. And so people with terminal illnesses get married. Prisoners in a concentration camp plant flowers. Lovers long divorced still reach out in the night to embrace one who is no longer there. It's like the phantom pain experienced by those who have lost a limb. Feelings still emanate from that region where once was a crucial part of them, and they will sometimes find themselves being careful not to bang the corner of a table or slam the car door on a leg or an arm long since removed. Our hearts know a similar reality. At some deep level, we refuse to accept the fact that this is the way things are, or must be, or always will be.

Simone Weil was right; there are only two things that pierce the human heart: beauty and affliction. Moments we wish would last forever and moments we wish had never begun. What are we to make of these messengers? How are we to interpret what they are saying? The playwright Christopher Fry writes,

> The inescapable dramatic situation for us all is that we have no idea what our situation is. We may be mortal. What then? We

may be immortal. What then? We are plunged into an existence fantastic to the point of nightmare, and however hard we
rationalize, or however firm our religious faith, however closely
we dog the heels of science or wheel among the starts of mysticism, we cannot really make head or tail of it. ("A Playwright
Speaks: How Lost, How Amazed, How Miraculous We Are")

And what does Fry say we do with our dilemma? The worst
of all possible reactions:

> We get used to it. We get broken into it so gradually we
> scarcely notice it.

THE SAME OLD THING

Something awful has happened; something terrible. Something worse, even, than the fall of man. For in that greatest of all
tragedies, we merely lost Paradise—and with it, everything that
made life worth living. What has happened since is unthinkable:
we've gotten used to it. We're broken in to the idea that this is
just the way things are. The people who walk in great darkness
have adjusted their eyes. Regardless of our religious or philosophical beliefs, most of us live as though this life is pretty much
the way things are supposed to be. We dismiss the whispers of
joy with a cynical "Been there, done that, bought the T-shirt."
That way we won't have to deal with the haunting.

I was just talking with some friends about summer vacations, and I recommended that they visit the Tetons. "Oh,
yeah, we've been there. Nice place." Dismissal. And we
deaden our sorrows with cynicism as well, sporting a bumper
sticker that says, "Life sucks. Then you die." Then we try to

get on with life. We feed the cat, pay the bills, watch the news, and head off to bed, so we can do it all again tomorrow.

Standing before the open fridge, I'm struck by what I've just watched. Famine in Africa. Genocide . . . where? Someplace I can't even pronounce. I think it used to be part of the Soviet bloc. Corruption in Washington. Life as usual. It always ends with the anchor folding his notes and offering a pleasant "Good night." Good night? That's it? You have nothing else to say? You've just regaled us with the horrors of the world we live in, and all you can say is "Good night"? To be fair, he did promise more details—with film—at eleven. Just once I wish he would pause at the close of his report, take a long, deep breath, and then say, "How far we are from home," or "If only we had listened," or "Thank God, our sojourn here is drawing to an end." It never happens. I doubt it ever will. And not one of us gives it a second thought. It's just the way things are. Anytime I ask my neighbor how life is going, he always replies, "Same old thing."

Think with me for a moment. How has life turned out differently from the way you thought it would? If you are single, did you want to be? If you are married, is this the marriage you hoped for? Do you long to have children, or in having them, are you delighted with the course they've chosen for their lives? Your friendships—are they as rich and deep and lasting as you want? When the holidays roll around, do you look forward with eager anticipation to the time you'll spend with the people in your life? And afterward, as you pack away the decorations and clean up the mess, did the reality match your expectations?

How about your work, your place in the world—do you go to bed each night with a deep sense of having made a lasting contribution? Do you enjoy ongoing recognition for your unique successes? Are you even working in a field that fits you? Are you working at all? Now, what if I told you that this is how it will always be, that this life as you now experience it will go on forever just as it is, without improvement of any kind? Your health will stay as it is, your finances will remain as they are, your relationships, your work, all of it.

It is hell.

IN DEFENSE OF DISCONTENT

By the grace of God, we cannot quite pull it off. In the quiet moments of the day we sense a nagging within, a discontent, a hunger for something else. But because we have not solved the riddle of our existence, we assume that something is wrong—not with life, but with us. *Everyone else seems to be getting on with things. What's wrong with me?* We feel guilty about our chronic disappointment. *Why can't I just learn to be happier in my job, in my marriage, in my church, in my group of friends?* You see, even while we are doing other things, "getting on with life," we still have an eye out for the life we secretly want. When someone seems to have gotten it together, we wonder, *How did he do it?* Maybe if we read the same book, spent time with him, went to his church, things would come together for us as well. We can never entirely give up our quest. May reminds us,

> When the desire is too much to bear, we often bury it beneath frenzied thoughts and activities or escape it by dulling our immediate consciousness of living. It is possible to run away from the desire for years, even decades, at a time, but we cannot eradicate it entirely. It keeps touching us in little glimpses and hints in our dreams, our hopes, our unguarded moments. (*The Awakened Heart*)

He says that even though we sleep, our desire does not. "It is who we are." We *are* desire. It is the essence of the human soul, the secret of our existence. Absolutely nothing of human greatness is ever accomplished without it. Not a symphony has been written, a mountain climbed, an injustice fought, or a love sustained apart from desire. Desire fuels our search for the life we prize. Our desire, if we will listen to it, will save us from committing soul-suicide, the sacrifice of our hearts on the altar of "getting by." The same old thing is not enough. It never will be.

The secret that begins to solve the riddle of our lives is simply this: we are the sea lion who lost the sea. Life as usual is not the life we truly want. It is not the life we truly need. It is not the life we were made for. If we would only listen to our hearts, to what G. K. Chesterton called our "divine discontent," we would learn the secret of our existence. As he wrote in *Orthodoxy*, "We have come to the wrong star . . . That is what makes life at once so splendid and so strange. The true happiness is that we *don't* fit. We come from somewhere else. We have lost our way."

The meaning of our lives is revealed through experiences that at first seem at odds with each other—moments we wish would never end and moments we wish had never begun. Those timeless experiences we want to last forever whisper to us that *they were meant to*. We were made to live in a world of beauty and wonder, intimacy and adventure all our days. Nathaniel Hawthorne insisted, "Our Creator would never have made such lovely days, and given us the deep hearts to enjoy them, above and beyond all thought, unless we were meant to be immortal."

There is more to these days than pictures tucked away in photo albums, fading as the memory fades from view. We use a statement to try to console ourselves with what we think is the irrecoverable loss: "All good things come to an end." I hate that phrase. It's a lie. Even our troubles and our heartbreaks tell us something about our true destiny. The tragedies that strike us to the core and elicit the cry, "This isn't the way it was supposed to be!" are also telling the truth—it *isn't* the way it was supposed to be. Pascal writes,

> Man is so great that his greatness appears even in knowing himself to be miserable. A tree has no sense of its misery. It is true that to know we are miserable is to be miserable; but to know we are miserable is also to be great. Thus all the miseries of man prove his grandeur; they are the miseries of a dignified personage, the miseries of a dethroned monarch . . . What can this incessant craving, and this impotence of attainment mean, unless there was once a happiness belonging to man, of which only the faintest traces remain, in that void which he attempts to fill with everything within his reach? (*Pensées*)

Should the king in exile pretend he is happy there? Should he not seek his own country? His miseries are his ally; they urge him on. Let them grow, if need be. But do not forsake the secret of life; do not despise those kingly desires. We abandon the most important journey of our lives when we abandon desire. We leave our hearts by the side of the road and head off in the direction of fitting in, getting by, being productive, what have you. Whatever we might gain—money, position, the approval of others, or just absence of the discontent itself—it's not worth it. "What good will it be for a man if he gains the whole world, yet forfeits his soul?" (Matt. 16:26 NIV).

TAKING UP THE QUEST

We must return to the journey. Wherever we are, whatever we are doing, we must pick up the trail and follow the map that we have at hand. Desire, both the whispers and the shouts, is the map we have been given to find the only life worth living. You may think you are following the map of desire when all you are doing is serving it slavishly, unthinkingly. It is not the same. We must *listen* to desire, look at it carefully, let it guide us through the false routes and dead ends. C. S. Lewis advises us,

> I knew only too well how easily the longing accepts false objects and through what dark ways the pursuit of them leads us. But I also saw that the Desire itself contains the corrective of all these errors. The only fatal error was to pretend you had passed from desire to fruition, when, in reality, you had found either nothing, or desire itself, or the satisfaction of some different desire. The dialectic of Desire, faithfully followed, would retrieve all mistakes, head you off from all false paths, and force you to live through . . . a sort of [experiential] proof. (*The Pilgrim's Regress*)

The only fatal error is to pretend that we have found the life we prize. To mistake the water hole for the sea. To settle for the same old thing. Fry called such a life "the sleep of prisoners." You might remember the movie *The Shawshank Redemption*, the story of prison life in the Northeast in the 1940s. The film focuses on the journey of two men's hearts through the trials and temptations of incarceration. Red, the ringleader and most seasoned of the prisoners, explains what happens when you live within those walls too long: "At first, these walls, you hate them. They make you crazy. After a while you get used to 'em, don't notice 'em anymore. Then comes the day you realize you need them." That is the most tragic day of all—to prefer slavery to freedom, to prefer death to life. We must not stay in this sleep. The time has come for us to wake, to arise from our slumber. As the Scriptures say, "Wake up, O sleeper, rise from the dead" (Eph. 5:14 NIV). And so MacDonald prayed,

> When I can no more stir my soul to move,
> And life is but the ashes of a fire;
> When I can but remember that my heart
> Once used to live and love, long and aspire—
> Oh, be thou then the first, the one thou art;
> Be thou the calling, before all answering love,
> And in me wake hope, fear, boundless desire.
>
> (*Diary of an Old Soul*)

Bringing our heart along in our life's journey is the most important mission of our lives—and the hardest. It all turns on what we do with our desire. If you will look around, you will see that most people have abandoned the journey. They have lost heart. They are camped in places of resignation or indulgence, or trapped in prisons of despair. I understand; I have frequented all those places before and return to them even still. Life provides any number of reasons and occasions to abandon desire. Certainly, one of the primary reasons is that it creates for us our deepest dilemmas. To desire something and not to have it—is this not the source of nearly all our pain and sorrow?

ALSO AVAILABLE FROM JOHN ELDREDGE

Wild at Heart: A Band of Brothers.

Five friends. Eight days. No scripts. Here's what it looks like to live the message of *Wild at Heart* in a band of real brothers. John and his band of brothers spent eight days shooting this series on a ranch in Colorado. Horses. Rappelling, Whitewater rafting. Fly-fishing. And some of the most honest conversation you will ever hear from men. This is not a scripted instructional video. It is real life and conversation shared with the cameras rolling. If you're looking for more, this is the next step in the *Wild at Heart* adventure for you and your band of brothers. The Multi-Media Facilitator's Kit includes John's best-selling *Wild at Heart* hardcover book; the *Wild at Heart Field Manual;* the *Wild at Heart Facilitator's Guide;* the video teaching series available either in VHS or DVD format; and a media kit to help you get the word out so others can join your band of brothers.

VHS—ISBN 1-4002-0087-3

DVD—ISBN 1-4002-0086-5

Wild at Heart

Every man was once a boy. And every little boy has dreams, big dreams. But what happens to those dreams when they grow up? In *Wild at Heart*, John Eldredge invites men to recover their masculine heart, defined in the image of a passionate God. And he invites women to discover the secret of a man's soul and to delight in the strength and wildness men were created to offer.

Hardcover—ISBN 0-7852-6883-9

Abridged Audio in 3 CDs—ISBN 0-7852-6298-9

Abridged Audio in 2 cassettes—ISBN 0-7852-6498-1

Spanish Edition (*Salvaje de Corazón*)—ISBN 0-8811-3716-2

Wild at Heart Field Manual

Abandoning the format of workbooks-as-you-know-them, the *Wild at Heart Field Manual* will take you on a journey through which you will receive permission to be what God designed you to be—dangerous, passionate, alive, and free. Filled with questions, exercises, personal stories from readers, wide-open writing spaces to record your "field notes," this book will lead you on a journey to discover the masculine heart that God gave you.

ISBN 0-7852-6574-0

The Wild at Heart Journal.

This rugged leather-bound guided journey will help men explore their hearts and journal their adventures. This includes totally different material than that found in the *Field Manual*.
ISBN 0-8499-5763-X

The Three Classics:

The Sacred Romance, The Journey of Desire, and *Wild at Heart* are available in one specially priced package. Whether this special set is for yourself, to replace the dog-eared and penciled-in copies you already own, or is a gift to share John's powerful message with someone you love, these *Three Classics from John Eldredge* will continue to give long after they are received.
ISBN 0-7852-6635-6

The Sacred Romance

This life-changing book by Brent Curtis and John Eldredge has guided hundreds of thousands of readers from a busyness-based religion to a deeply felt relationship with the God who woos you. As you draw closer to Him, you must choose to let go of other "less-wild lovers," such as perfectionistic drivenness and self-indulgence, and embark on your own journey to recover the lost life of your heart and with it the intimacy, beauty, and adventure of life with God.
Trade Paper Edition—ISBN 0-7852-7342-5
Special Collector's Edition (Hardcover)—ISBN 0-7852-6723-9
Abridged Audio in 2 Cassettes—ISBN 0-7852-6786-7
Spanish Edition (*El Sagrado Romance*)—ISBN 0-8811-3648-4

The Sacred Romance Workbook and Journal

John Eldredge offers a guided journey of the heart featuring exercises, journaling, and the arts to usher you into an *experience*—the recovery of your heart and the discovery of your life as part of God's great romance.
ISBN 0-7852-6846-4

The Journey of Desire

Author Dan Allender calls *The Journey of Desire* "a profound and winsome call to walk into the heart of God." This life-changing book picks up where *The Sacred Romance* leaves off and continues the journey. In it, John Eldredge invites you to abandon resignation, to rediscover your God-given desires, and to search again for the life you once dreamed of.
Hardcover Edition—ISBN 0-7852-6882-0
Trade Paper Edition—ISBN 0-7852-6716-6

The Journey of Desire Journal and Guidebook
John Eldredge, with Craig McConnell, offers a unique, thought-provoking, and life-recapturing workbook, which invites you to rediscover your God-given desire and to search again for the life you once dreamed of. Less of a workbook and more of a flowing journal, this book includes personal responses to questions from John and Craig.
ISBN 0-7852-6640-2

Dare to Desire
Complete with beautiful, full-color design, *Dare to Desire* is the perfect book if you are ready to move beyond the daily grind to a life overflowing with adventure, beauty, and a God who loves you more passionately than you dared imagine. With brand-new content as well as concepts from *The Sacred Romance*, *The Journey of Desire*, and *Wild at Heart*, John Eldredge takes you on a majestic journey through the uncharted waters of the human heart.
ISBN 0-8499-9591-4

Waking the Dead.
In *Waking the Dead*, John Eldredge shows how God restores your heart, your true humanity, and sets you free. There are four streams, Eldredge says, through which you can discover the abundant life: Walking with God, Receiving His Intimate Counsel, Deep Restoration, and Spiritual Warfare. And once the "eyes of your heart" are opened, you will embrace three eternal truths: Things are not what they seem; This is a world at war; and You have a crucial role to play. A battle is raging. And it is a battle for your heart.
Hardcover—ISBN 0-7852-6553-8
Abridged Audio in 3 CDs—ISBN 0-7852-6299-7

A Guidebook to Waking the Dead:
Embracing the Life God Has for You.
In a style similar to *The Journey of Desire Journal and Guidebook*, Eldredge and Craig McConnell lead you on a journey toward a restored heart, true humanity, and ultimate freedom.
ISBN 0-7852-6309-8